The Hand of God

The Hand of God

Thoughts and Images Reflecting the Spirit of the Universe

Introductory Essay by Sharon Begley

Edited by Michael Reagan

Templeton Foundation Press
Philadelphia and London

The Hand of God

Copyright © 1999 Lionheart Books, LTD.
Images on pages 62-63,108-109,125 © 1999 John P. Gleason
Images on pages 6-7,39,48,50,112,114-115 © 1999 Jerry Lodriguss
Images on pages 37,49,56-57,160 © 1999 Jason Ware
Images on pages 2,26,40,51,52-53 © 1999 AAO/David Malin
All other digital images © 1999 Lionheart Books

First paperback edition.
First edition (hardcover) published by Andrews McMeel Publishing.
Printed in Italy. No part of this book may be used or reproduced in any manner
whatsoever without written permission except in the case of reprints in the context of
reviews. For information, write Templeton Foundation Press,
5 Radnor Corporate Center, Suite 120, Radnor, PA 19087.

www.templetonpress.org

01 02 03 04 TRC 10 9 8 7 6 5 4 3 2 1

Library of Congress Cataloging-in-Publication Data
The hand of God : a collection of thoughts and images reflecting the
spirit of the universe / introductory essay by Sharon Begley ;
edited by Michael Reagan.
p. cm.
ISBN: 1-890151-52-1
1. Religion and science. 2. Creation. I. Reagan, Michael, 1949-
BL240.2H36 1999
291.1'75—dc21   99-37232
CIP

Produced by Lionheart Books, Ltd.
5105 Peachtree Industrial Boulevard
Atlanta, Georgia 30341

Design: Carley Wilson Brown & Michael Reagan
Research : Gina Webb
Cover Image: Hubble Space Telescope/NASA/ESA

Foreword

This is a book I have been thinking about for a number of years— since I saw the first Hubble Telescope images. My overwhelming impression at that time was one of awe at the majesty of the universe and a sense that I was witnessing the hand of God at work on a scale that was mind-boggling. To me (and I think many others) these images are a catalyst leading us to ponder the "idea" of God. For some reason when I look at this material I have a great sense of relief, an almost surreal sense that it's all going to be OK, we are not alone, and there is a God.

Michael Reagan

We had the sky, up there, all speckled with stars, and we used to lay on our backs and look up at them, and discuss about whether they was made, or only just happened.

—MARK TWAIN
Huckleberry Finn

Comet Hale-Bopp *as it passes near the North American Nebula. The two tails of the comet are formed by material ejected from the nucleus. Gas ions are blue, and dust particles are white.*

Jerry Lodriguss

INTRODUCTION

Essay by Sharon Begley

Galileo/NASSA/JPL

Earth's Moon—*This image was taken by the Galileo spacecraft from a distance of about 75,000 miles through a violet filter as it passed over the north pole of the Moon.*

The age of naked-eye astronomy has lasted for most of our time on Earth: if the length of humankind's 2.5 million-year tenure is taken as one 24-hour day, then the era of the telescope has lasted a mere 15 seconds. Throughout the other 23 hours, 59 minutes and 45 seconds, our unaided eyes could no more penetrate the veils covering the secrets of the universe than the flash of a firefly could penetrate the canopy of stars that unfurled above us every cloudless night. Few people realized that, beyond the visible stars and moon and occasional planet, there lay worlds and worlds without end. But even though we could see no farther than the frontispiece of the universe, in the years before telescopes the cosmos still drew us. It was the stuff of eternity, infinity—as unbounded as humankind's imagination.

Come, the stars invited; lie supine at the top of a hill on a night when neither the glow of the moon nor a roof of clouds interferes with your view of the sky, in a place where the lights of human habitation are too dim to wash out the view. Look up. There, where the Pleiades burn. Or there—where Orion stretches so boldly over the southern sky. And everywhere, where the uncounted and uncountable hosts prick the black velvet. Look. Stare. Maybe the indifferent heavens will offer a sign, however small, that there is a world beyond the world we see, that there is meaning in the void and a harmony between the mind of man and the limitless reaches of space.

Closing the gaps of that limitless reach have been the 20th century's high-powered telescopes. Namesake of Hubble, remote offspring of Galileo, today's space-based machinery bring us images so far beyond what we could ever imagine that they have changed dramatically our view of the heavens and the origins of the universe. And yet, ironically, the more focused the portraits from deep space, the more meticulous and specific our calculations, the more it seems improbable, even impossible, that our world could have been an arbitrary occurrence.

The majesty of the heavens and their regularity—the cycling of the seasons, the rhythm of day and night—inspire a suspicion that we simply cannot be looking at some meaningless accident. How fitting, then, that it is in cosmology—the scientific study of the beginning and evolution of the universe—where the stage is set for a historic reconciliation of those two rivals for man's awe: science and religion. In the skies themselves, and in what cosmologists are learning about them, the armies of the mind and the forces of the spirit are searching for common ground.

To appreciate the seismic change taking place in the relationship between science and faith, one need only recall how deeply the rift between the two has become part of our culture. Walt Whitman captured it best when he wrote in the poem that was to become part of "Leaves of Grass,"

When I heard the learn'd astronomer,
When the proofs, the figures, were ranged in columns before me
When I was shown the charts and the diagrams, to add,
*   divide, and measure them;*
When I, sitting, heard the astronomer, where he lectured
*   with much applause in the lecture-room,*
How soon, unaccountable, I became tired and sick;
Till rising and gliding out, I wander'd off by myself,
In the mystical moist night-air, and from time to time,
Look'd up in perfect silence at the stars.

Whitman was not alone when he complained that "the learn'd astronomer's" discoveries had spoiled the mystery and romance of the stars; his poem describes the science most of us know. It is a science that has, traditionally, encroached on the terrain of religion, offering a natural (and often dry) explanation for what had previously been regarded as wondrous and even supernatural. It is a science that obliterates mysteries and replaces them with a differential equation. It is a science that addresses totally different questions than religion: Science explains the world, God is behind the world; science explains what is, religion offers a sense of what ought to be; science tells us how the world acts, religion tells us how we should act.

And yet it was not always so. For most of the previous 2,000 years, science and religion were engaged in a common quest for understanding, each taking strength from the other.

Until the middle of the 19th century, science was perceived not as antithetical to faith but rather as an avenue to deeper faith and to greater appreciation for the works of the Creator. In nature, scientists believed, could be discerned the handiwork of God.

The leading lights of the Scientific Revolution were men of faith as well as men of science. Early astronomers like Tycho Brahe and Johannes Kepler, devout Christians both, studied the motions of the planets and believed that, in so doing, they were getting a peek at the blueprints that God had drawn for the universe. Isaac Newton did not doubt that in uncovering the laws of motion and universal gravitation, he was being granted a glimpse of the operating manual of the vast machine called Creation that God had assembled and kept running.

These early scientists trusted that their inquiries would yield knowledge because they believed that God had created a rational, ordered world, a world governed by laws and not by chaos or divine whim, a world in which discoveries therefore had universal meaning: if an apple fell *here* for one reason, then that reason applied throughout the universe. The world was not an endless sequence of unique cases. Without the confidence that there existed a consistent, rational, eternal set of principles governing nature, there wouldn't be much point in doing science—whose goal is, after all, the uncovering of the regularities of nature that we have come to call laws.

In the 17th century, science and religion signed a sort of mutual nonaggression treaty, in which each vowed to refrain from spreading into the domain of the other. For science, this move was defensive: by declaring outright that its discoveries did not, and could not, be used as tools to undermine belief, science was declaring that it operated in a domain parallel to rather than overlapping that where religion reigned. This was partly a reaction to how the Church had treated Galileo. If science took the position that its discoveries did not speak to the truth or falsity of religion, there would be no more—or, at least, less excuse for—putting scientists under house arrest. For faith, a nonaggression treaty also offered protection: by asserting that it spoke to realities beyond the reach of science, it effectively inoculated itself from any surprise discoveries that might otherwise be interpreted as undermining its teachings.

But the rise of science had already brought with it Copernicus's Sun-centered solar system, which knocked Earth from the center of creation. Next came Newton's

physics, which made of the universe an inanimate wind-up machine. The Enlightenment's focus on reason as the supreme human power, its philosophies of reductionism and materialism, and its rejection of authority and revelation and text, were all antithetical to religion. The truce was fraying.

Saturn's System—*This montage of images was prepared from an assemblage of images taken by the Voyager 1 spacecraft. The artist's view shows Dione in the forefront, Saturn rising behind, Tethys and Mimas fading in the distance to the right, Enceladus and Rhea off Saturn's rings to the left, and Titan in its distant orbit at the top.*

In 1859 Charles Darwin published, in *On the Origin of Species*, his theory of evolutionary biology, which seemed to dethrone the Creator and replace him with blind chance. Darwin more than any scientist before dislodged humans from the apex of the tree of life, making them seem almost incidental to Creation, an afterthought, some meaningless bits of carbon chemistry dotting an insignificant planet orbiting an ordinary star way out in the hinterland of a galaxy indistinguishable from the other 100 billion galaxies believed to fill the universe. The biologist's view of life as a series of complex chemical reactions did not lie easily with the theologian's idea of life as a divine gift; if everything from the creation of the planets to the eruption of a volcano to the leukemia that takes the life of a child is seen as having, in fact or in theory, a natural cause and explanation, then it seemed like there was no room left for God to act in the world. Darwin's theory of evolution through natural selection was arguably the single event that allowed the supposedly unbridgeable chasm between God and science to attain the status of iconic truth.

From the mid-19th century on, the relationship between science and faith deteriorated into one of animosity, at least in the West. True, some theologians made their peace with modern science: one American clergyman welcomed Darwin's theory of evolution through chance and natural selection because that view implied that God had created a world that could and did make itself. This was a gift of love, the clergyman argued, allowing the

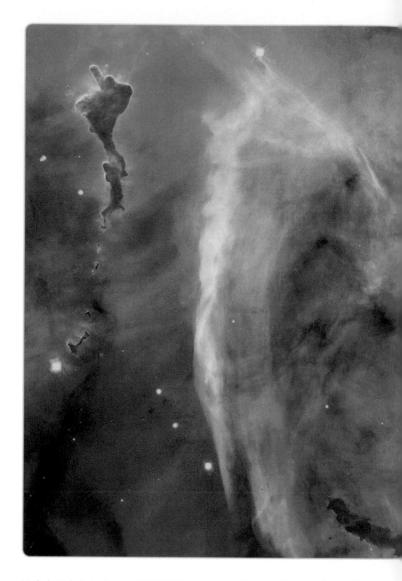

Keyhole Nebula in Carinia (NGC 3372)—*was named in the 19th century by Sir John Herschel. This region, about 8,000 light years from Earth, is located in the constellation Carina.*

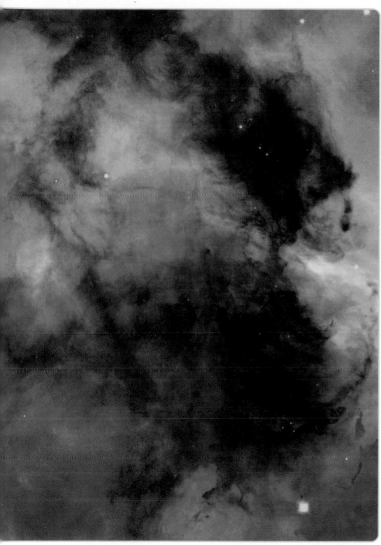

Hubble Heritage Team/AURA/STScI/NASA

The Carina Nebula also contains several other stars that are among the hottest and most massive known, each about 10 times hotter, and 100 times more massive, than our Sun.

creation to have independence rather than making it a divine puppet theater. But few men of God saw Darwin's theory in any such positive light. Instead, most other theologians began to identify science as the enemy, as a hostile force invading and laying waste to the sacred.

For centuries theologians had appealed to "the God of the gaps." This God is the one whom you offer in explanation for phenomena that otherwise have none. Did the rains come? God brought them (until meteorologists discovered how a specific combination of atmospheric pressure and humidity brings rain). Did the Sun rise? God lifted it (until astronomers figured out that Earth rotates on its axis once a day). Did life arise? God created it (until biologists discovered how abiotic molecules can replicate and evolve).

Thanks to the discoveries of 20th-century science, the gaps were growing ever fewer. It seemed that there was less and less for God to do. Astronomy and physics stepped in to explain that Earth formed when a disc of dust and gas spinning around the Sun condensed—another gap closed. Nuclear physics then came forward with an explanation for how stars burn through the fusion of hydrogen nuclei. Quantum mechanics, which was developed in the early 1900s, closed what had been considered the ultimate gap: the origins of the universe itself. This branch of physics has shown that there can be effects without causes, that material things can pop into and out of existence thanks to bizarre—but experimentally proven—phenomena called

Berlind & Challis/CfA/Wipple Observatory

quantum fluctuations. Quantum mechanics shook science's foundations to such an extent that even Einstein found its concepts intolerable. He argued the subject endlessly with fellow scientist Max Born: "The theory yields much, but it hardly brings us close to the secrets of the Old One," Einstein wrote in a letter to Born, adding his famous remark: "In any case, I am convinced that He does not play dice."

In the last few years cosmologists have offered a nearly airtight case that the universe itself could have originated naturally, not supernaturally, from the Big Bang. Even if few people could grasp the science on which this conclusion rested, its implications were clear—and deeply unsettling. Theoretical physicist Stephen Hawking, who has done much to popularize the new physics, put the question most succinctly: "So long as the universe had a beginning, we could suppose it had a Creator. But if the universe is really completely self-contained, what place, then, for a Creator?"

What place, indeed. The more science invaded the turf traditionally reserved for religion, offering a natural explanation for what had previously been regarded as divine, the less the God of the Gaps seemed to show Himself. He was no longer even necessary to explain Creation itself.

Bubbles and Arcs in NGC 2359—*A wind-blown shell nebula around the Wolf-Rayet star HD 56925, which is the bright star located at the center of the main bubble. Wolf-Rayet stars are massive, highly luminous stars that constantly cast off material in the stellar wind, which then commonly forms bubbles. But the unusual structure of the arcs indicates that something more is going on, although scientists are not sure what.*

With the scythe of science slashing away at all evidence of the divine, no wonder so many people have come to view science as nihilistic, as threatening, as undermining their hope that there is meaning in their lives, as replacing a sense of being unique and God-created with an existential void. This view was famously summed up by Nobel Prize-winning physicist Steven Weinberg, who concluded, "The more the universe seems comprehensible, the more it seems pointless."

Or maybe not. There is another interpretation of the understanding we have achieved. This view holds, contrary to Weinberg, that humankind's very ability to comprehend the universe suggests a profound connection, heretofore lost, between the mind of man and the works of God. Just as science once threatened faith, now it is—at least for some—restoring faith by offering this solace. For others, science is at least serving a function that faith alone once did: making humans feel connected to, not alienated from, creation.

The aspect of science that offers this hope is so basic that it is like Poe's purloined letter: right under our noses, we overlook it. This is the remarkable fact that the human mind can do science in the first place—that it can, in other words, figure out the world. Science works. Lights turn on when we flick a switch; buildings stand; water boils when we heat it; planets show up in the predicted place in space when we send robotic emissaries to them.

Why should this be so? "The magic of science is that we can understand at least part of nature—perhaps in principle all of it—using the scientific method of inquiry," says astronomer and physicist Paul Davies, winner of the Templeton Prize for advancing religion. Why, Davies asks, should the laws of nature be comprehensible and accessible to humans? It could, of course, be just a quirk, a coincidence, with no deeper meaning. Or, it could say something purely scientific—though we don't know, precisely, what—about the kind of beings that emerge from nature: as children of what Davies calls "the cosmic order," perhaps it is inevitable that their minds should "reflect that order in their cognitive capabilities."

Some scientists and theologians suspect, however, that the harmony between the intellectual ability of man and the laws of nature reflects something more profound. It need not be anything so simplistic as, "God made the world, and God made me, so He made me able to understand the rest of His Creation." It is, instead, one of those places where a scientific discovery—that the universe can be fathomed by the mind of man—serves a function that, once, only religion could. To wit: a sense of connectedness between humans and the cosmos.

The late Princeton University physicist and Nobel Prize winner Eugene Wigner called the ability to understand the world through the pure thought manifested in math "the unreasonable effectiveness of mathematics in the natural sciences." Wigner was referring to the superb, almost eerie, fit between what the human mind invents, out of pure thought, and the way the world works. It was human imagination—in this case Albert Einstein's—that invented general relativity, which turns out to describe the real world precisely. It was the human mind—physicist Paul Dirac's—that deduced, from pure mathematics, the existence of anti-matter, which had never been detected experimentally. A world with what physicist-turned-Anglican-minister John Polkinghorne calls such "rational transparency," is a world shot through, he says, "with signs of mind, and therefore Mind." This consonance between the mind of man and the workings of the universe implies, to some, a correspondence between us and it that a more nihilistic interpretation of science severed.

A second sort of cosmological discovery can also be interpreted in a way that supports belief. This is the finding that if the laws of physics were tweaked ever slightly, the world as we see it would not exist. With just tiny changes in the values of some of the numbers that go into the laws, no one would be around to marvel and wonder at any of this. The cosmos seems fine-tuned for existence, in an almost-too-good-to-be-true manner. To some, this "fine-tuning" of the laws that govern the universe is no less than proof of a designer.

Dumbbell Nebula NGC 6853 *was the first planetary nebula ever discovered. It has an estimated age of 3,000 to 4,000 years and is about 1,200 light years away. It is in the constellation Vulpecula. This false color depicts glowing hydrogen gas (green) and dense molecular gas and dust (red).*

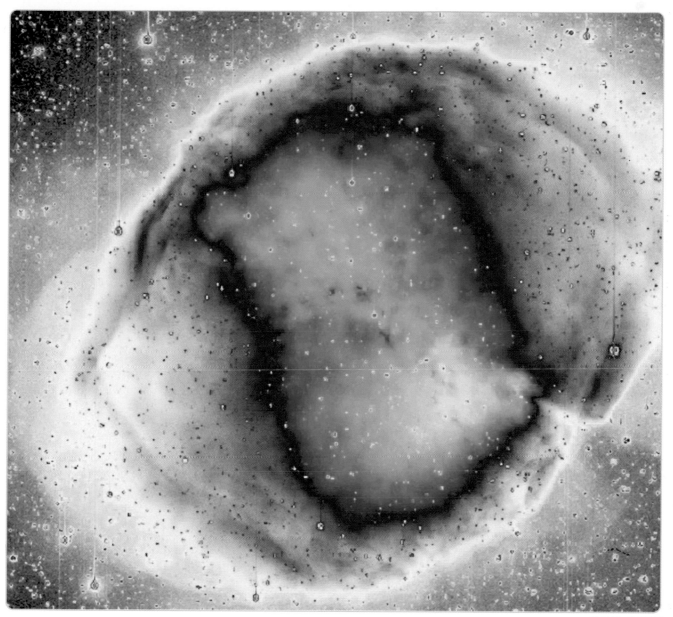

J.C. Cuillandre/CFHT

But one needn't go that far. The precise fit between the laws and constants of nature, on the one hand, and the existence of a universe and its inhabitants, on the other, simply inspires, in some people, a feeling that we are not isolated in the sea of time and space, but are intimately, integrally, tied to the universe—that we are, in fact, its expression. That's not the same thing as a personal relationship with God, let alone evidence of a God that cares about individuals, but it does bring some of the same solace and spiritual comfort as traditional religion. Even for non-believers, this fine-tuning is at minimum a source of wonder and awe.

Consider some examples of fine-tuning. If the strength of gravity were slightly greater than it is, the balls of gas that condensed into stars would keep collapsing until they quickly formed black holes. These collapsed stars are so dense, and their gravitational force therefore so powerful, that not even light can escape their pull. They are not very good for bathing any orbiting planets in life-giving warmth, as they emit neither heat nor light. Thus, if gravity were stronger than it is, neither our Sun nor we would be here. If the force of gravity were even a little weaker, then stars like the Sun would not be able to hold their planetary retinue in orbit; the planets would spiral out like a tether ball breaking off from its rope.

Another example: if a star is massive enough, it can die by exploding, a phenomenon called a supernova. The explosion scatters stardust—atomic elements that have been cooked up in the nuclear fires of the dying star—near and far. Most of the mass of the universe is in the form of the lightest elements that atoms can form, hydrogen and helium. But in burning stars, hydrogen and helium are forged into heavier elements, including oxygen, lithium, carbon and iron. These elements stream into space, eventually finding their way into spinning clouds of gas and dust out of which planets like Earth coalesce. The heavy elements escape the supernova only because of the existence of a ghostly subatomic particle called the neutrino. If neutrinos interacted just a bit less with other matter, they would not have been able to blast the heavy elements out of the supernova. The heavy elements would have hung around the cinder of the supernova like animals reluctant to leave their burned-out home, and the spinning disk of dust and gas out of which the Sun and Earth condensed five billion years ago would have been nothing but hydrogen and helium—which is hardly an impressive list of ingredients for a solid planet, let alone for life. In other words: If the mass of the neutrino were not precisely tuned, there would be no Earth-like planets and hence no life as we know it. We are indeed the children of stardust, stardust powered on its journey through the cosmos on the wind of neutrinos.

The fine-tuning doesn't end there. Life is carbon-based. Carbon is one of the elements cooked up, from helium, inside stars through nuclear fusion. Yet the recipe for carbon is as unforgiving of error as the most finicky soufflé instruction, as British astronomer Fred Hoyle discovered in

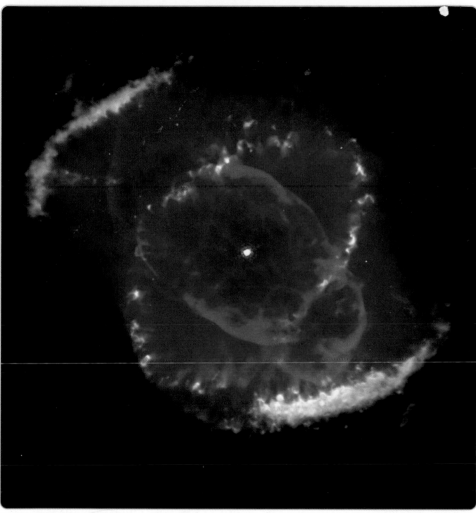

Hubble Space Telescope/NASA/ESA

Cat's Eye Nebula, NGC 6543 *is one of the most complex planetary nebulae ever seen. Estimated to be 1,000 years old, the nebula is a visual "fossil record" of a dying star. Planetary nebulae are created when dying stars lose outer layers of gas, forming cocoons. The process has nothing to do with planet formation, which is predicted to happen early in a star's life. NGC 6543 is 3,000 light years away in the constellation Draco.*

the 1960s. To form carbon, three of the helium nuclei whizzing around a star need to collide simultaneously—same place, same time. That occurs even less frequently with nuclei than it does with three friends meeting at a multiplex: it just doesn't happen that the three of you show up at precisely the same moment. But when the carbon nuclei have a specific energy, called a resonance, the chance of a triple encounter rises significantly, much as three friends are more likely to assemble at the same instant if they all step off the same bus at the same time and walk at the same speed to their rendezvous point.

Hoyle called this a "monstrous series of accidents," as if "the laws of nuclear physics have been deliberately designed with regard to the consequences they produce inside the stars." Because of this and similar "coincidences," Hoyle joked, the universe looks like a "put-up job." Someone has been turning the dials that determine the size of the gravitational constant and the strength of the force that glues together atomic nuclei, the strength of the electrical force and the masses of the fundamental particles—and frozen the knobs

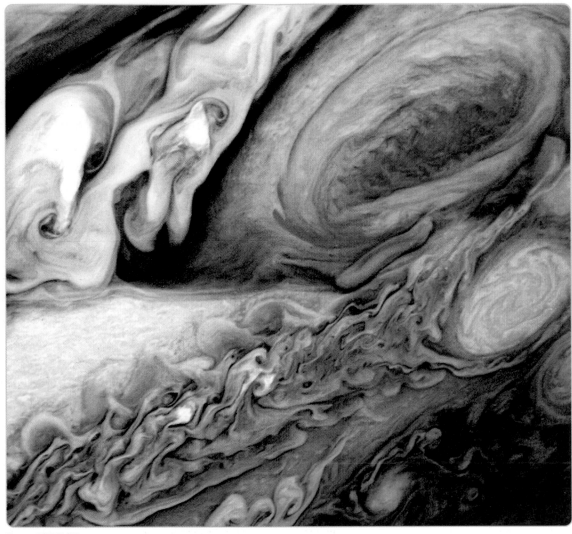

Voyager 1/NASA/JPL

Jupiter—*This exaggerated color image taken by Voyager 1 shows the Great Red Spot and the surrounding clouds. The Great Red Spot is about 12,000 kilometers across.*

at just the precise points that will lead to stars, and planets, and life intelligent enough to wonder about it all.

The idea that evidence of design in the universe—or structures that the human mind could not conceive as arising naturally—proves the existence of a designer has been pretty much left behind, along with the Middle Ages and Saint Augustine, whose treatise on the argument from design still stands as the exemplar of this kind of reasoning. But if design is not taken as proof, or even evidence, how is it interpreted? The answer varies with the individual, of course, since there is nothing more personal than faith. But one interpretation is this: the discoveries of fine-tuning and of the ability of the human mind to fathom the secrets of creation both nurture a faith that is already present. They allow believers, or those teetering on the edge between agnosticism and belief, to come down on one side. It provides an additional basis for belief.

One scientist whose research led him to faith is Alan Sandage, the astronomer who has spent the better part of the past forty years at the great telescopes on Mt. Wilson and Las Campanas Observatories. Sandage inherited the mantle of Edwin Hubble, who in 1929 discovered that the universe is expanding, rushing out like a tide and carrying along with it galaxies and nebulas like so much flotsam and jetsam upon the waves of spacetime. After Hubble's death in 1953, Sandage assumed the task of measuring the fate of the universe.

To do so, Sandage observed two kinds of stars: exploded stars called supernovas and variable stars called Cepheids, whose period of variation in brightness and intrinsic luminosity are precisely related. Sandage determined the distance to these stars by the shift in their light spectra, and calculated their recession velocity. The relationship between those two numbers would reveal whether the universe would expand forever or, one day, stop and reverse course, hurtling toward a Big Crunch. For the insights they gave him into the design of the cosmos, Sandage called the photographic plates that he and others made at Palomar's telescopes "the plates of Moses."

As much as any other 20th-century astronomer, Sandage actually figured out the Creation: his observations showed how old the universe is (15 billion years or so) and that it is expanding just fast enough to do so forever. But throughout it all Sandage was nagged by mysteries whose answers were not to be found in the glittering supernovas. Among them: Why is there something rather than nothing? He began to despair of answering such questions through reason alone. "It was my science that drove me to the conclusion that the world is much more complicated than can be explained by science," he says. "It is only through the supernatural that I can understand the mystery of existence."

Some scientists who study not the macro-world of astronomy but the micro-world of particles smaller than an atom have been similarly moved. Quantum mechanics, the branch of physics that describes events at the subatomic level, is a consistent, empirically proved framework that predicts how subatomic particles behave and interact. But it is also "spooky," to use Einstein's description. His most famous experiment in this regard is so odd that, when Einstein devised it with two collaborators as a thought experiment in 1935, he called it a paradox. It goes like this. Let's say that a radioactive atom decays. In so doing, it emits a pair of particles. The particles are linked forever in this way: the laws of nature dictate that if one of the particles is spinning in a way that we can call clockwise, then the other particle is spinning counterclockwise.

Now, let's say that you measure the spin of one of the particles. It turns up clockwise. By this very act of measurement, then, you have *determined* the spin of the other

Spiral Galaxy NGC 4603—*This Hubble Space Telescope image is the most distant galaxy in which Cepheid variable stars (a rare class of pulsating stars that are used to determine distances) have been found. NGC 4603, which is associated with the Centaurus cluster, one of the most massive assemblages of galaxies in the nearby universe, was determined to be 108 million light years away. This measurement has helped provide a precise calculation of the universe's expansion rate, called the Hubble Constant, which is crucial to determining the age of the universe.*

particle—even if it is at the other end of the universe. Einstein called this "spooky action at the distance," but it has been proved right time and again. What happens, according to physicists' current interpretation, is that each particle exists in two states simultaneously, somehow spinning clockwise and counterclockwise at the same time. Only when an observer makes a measurement on one particle does that particle settle down and choose one spin. This choice affects which spin its partner chooses. This suggests to some scholars a level of reality beyond the familiar everyday one, a reality in which spatial distance is meaningless (because the second particle receives the information about the first particle's choice simultaneously and makes its own choice based on that instantaneously). It is in this other level of reality that some find a place for the existence of a supreme being.

Cygnus Loop Nebula—*A small portion of the nebula which is actually the expanding blastwave from a stellar cataclysm— a supernova explosion—which occurred about 15,000 years ago. This supernova remnant lies 2,500 light years away in the constellation Cygnus the Swan.*

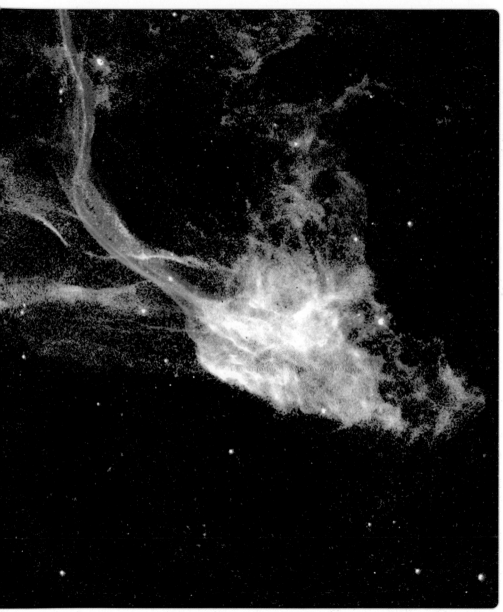

Twentieth-century discoveries in astronomy and cosmology—"the charts and the diagrams," to say nothing of the formulas and calculations—are not sending us "tired and sick," fleeing like Whitman back into the mysteries of "the moist night" to take refuge in our ignorance. Instead, astronomers' findings—both the new nebulae and novas and galaxies they spy with their telescopes and the inferences they draw about the orbs scattered across the universe—are restoring a sense of wonder, and even of purpose, in a world at times hostile to both. Instead of leaving less and less room for a Creator who, at least once, acted in the world, they are acting as an inspiration to and support for faith.

This is a momentous switch. Science has been pilloried for centuries for robbing the world of its enigmatic beauty and for squeezing God out of the picture. Like kudzu creeping over the

landscape of the South, it spread into the realm of religion until there was not a patch of territory that religion could claim as its own. Finally, science, the bogeyman of faith, is undergoing a radical change in its place in human culture.

And so it is hardly surprising that scholars of a certain ideology regard all of this harmonizing and reconciliation between science and theology as misguided at best and dangerous at worst. One objection is that when physicists, cosmologists, and other scientists throw around the word "God," they do not mean what most people mean. In the scientists' usage, "God" stands for some abstract, ineffable principle of order and physical law. But it definitely does not mean a being who cares for, and even intervenes in the lives of, human beings. Even if it is not the God of the Old Testament, interacting with people and reaching down into their lives at the drop of a plague, then He is at least a personal God, omniscient and omnipotent, who acts in the world. This is not, one must admit, the God that cosmologists or other scientists are finding.

Another trouble with claiming to find parallels between the discoveries of science and the tenets of a specific religion is that if every faith finds support in science, then none of them can truly claim to. It becomes a case of finding only what you seek. Also, scientists know all too well how tentative and subject to change science is: if people of faith

Corona Australis Nebula NGC 6726-27-29—*This spectacular reflection nebula is the result of a few bright stars caught up in a large, dusty cloud. The dark cloud appears to be an active star-forming nebula.*

derive inspiration and even worldviews based on a particular cosmological model, what happens when science overthrows that model, in favor of a more accurate one, as it inevitably does? Belief should not be held hostage to the shifting truths of science.

Among those suspicious of any reconciliation, Stephen Jay Gould, the Harvard University paleontologist and historian of science, calls science and religion "non-overlapping magisteria," by which he means domains that address such totally separate questions that they should never even intersect. In his view, which is shared by many scientists, nature is regally indifferent to human welfare and human yearnings, whether for meaning, or enlightenment, or even a sense of connection to an entity larger and more enduring than the self. To this way of thinking, any attempt at reconciliation is folly, or even pernicious, weakening the majesty of religion and the authority of science.

But the discoveries that come streaming in from our telescopes are inspiring thoughtful people not to subsume science to faith or faith to science, but to seek an accommodation between the two. It is this quest that is winning adherents as the millennium begins. Science and religion illuminate different mysteries, all agree, casting their light on different questions. But each can heal the worst excesses of the other, with science, as Pope Paul II said, "purify[ing] religion from error and superstition," and religion "purify[ing] science from idolatry and false absolutes" by infusing it with a little humility. Or, as

Einstein observed, "Science without religion is lame, religion without science is blind."

The new scholarship of science and theology suggests, too, that they have one thing in common: the motivation that animates both in the search for scientific truths and the search for spiritual meaning. "I think that fundamentally the impetus for the two quests is the same," says Carl Feit, a biologist and practicing Jew. "Religion and science are two ways of looking at the world, and each helps guide our search for understanding. Profoundly religious people are asking the same questions as profound scientists: Who are we? And what are we? What's the purpose? What's the end? Where do we come from? And where are we going? We have this need, this desire, this drive, to understand ourselves and the world that we live in."

When Václav Havel, the poet and president of the Czech Republic, received the Liberty Medal in Philadelphia on the 218th anniversary of the Declaration of Independence, he described the societal transition underway in the world. Science, he said, has become alienated from the lives we lead. For too long it has failed "to connect with the most intrinsic nature of reality and with natural human experience. It is now more a source of disintegration and doubt than a source of integration and meaning." But he saw a glimmer of hope. "Paradoxically, inspiration for the renewal of this lost integrity can once again be found in science . . . a science producing ideas that in a certain sense allow it to transcend its own limits. . . . Transcendence is the only real alternative to extinction," especially the extinction of the collective human soul. That was in 1994. Now, as the millennium turns, Havel's hope that science would cease to be a source of doubt and become a source of inspiration is becoming realized.

At the end of the 20th century, it is in what science is unearthing about nature that we are seeing confirmation of existing religious beliefs or inspiration for a whole new kind of faith. We are not fusing religion and science; the two will always retain their separate identities. But from scholars to churchgoers to those who have turned their backs on organized religion, we are seeking and finding today in the discoveries of science—and especially in the discoveries of astronomy and cosmology—what in eras past only religion has offered: solace and support. A sense of connection between the otherwise insignificant human mind and the tapestry of creation. A sense of wonder, and of awe; a sense that the world is rational; a sense, even, of the sacred. And, to believers, hints of the nature and character of God.

Glowing Pool Of Light—NGC 3132 *is a striking example of a planetary nebula. This expanding cloud of gas, surrounding a dying star, is known in the southern hemisphere as the "Eight-Burst" or the "Southern Ring" Nebula. It is nearly 1/2 light year in diameter and 2,000 light years away. The image shows two stars near the center of the nebula, a bright white one and a fainter companion to its upper left. It is actually the faint partner that has ejected the nebula.*

Hubble Heritage Team/AURA/STScI/NASA

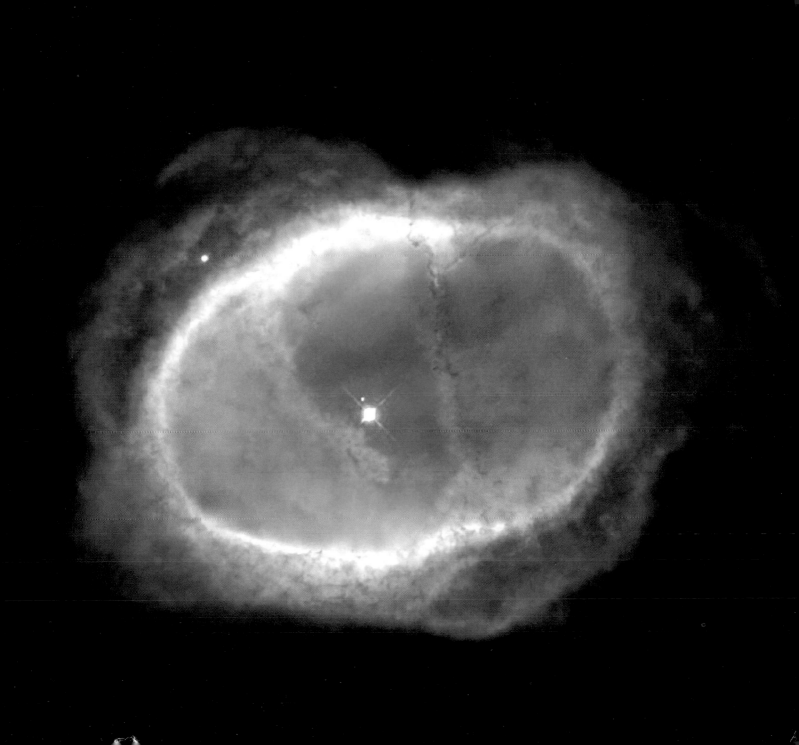

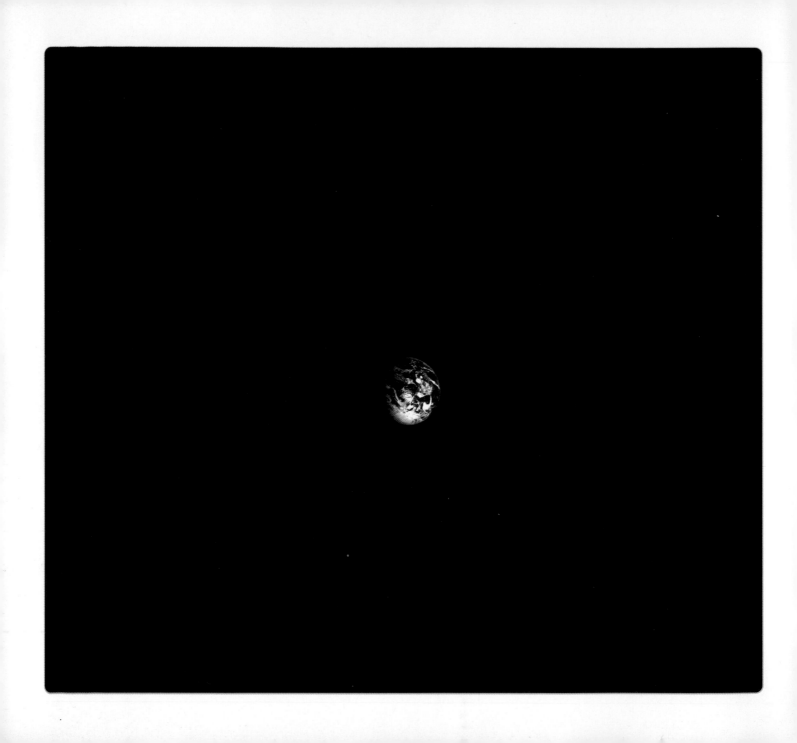

"I say!" murmured Horton. *"I've never heard tell*
Of a small speck of dust that is able to yell.
So you know what I think? . . . Why, I think that there must
Be someone on top of that small speck of dust!"

—DR. SEUSS
Horton Hears a Who

My religion consists of a humble admiration of the illimitable superior spirit who reveals himself in the slight details we are able to perceive with our frail and feeble minds. That deeply emotional conviction of the presence of a superior reasoning power, which is revealed in the incomprehensible universe, forms my idea of God.

✝ ALBERT EINSTEIN ✝

Star Birth in NGC 1850— *166,000 light years away in the Large Magellanic Cloud (LMC) galaxy. There are nearly 10,000 stars in three separate populations. About 60% are in a cluster called NGC 1850, estimated to be 50 million years old. Another cluster of about 20% is only 4 million years old.*

I find it quite improbable that such order came out of chaos. There has to be some organizing principle. God to me is a mystery but is the explanation for the miracle of existence, why there is something instead of nothing.

ALAN SANDAGE
Winner of the Crawford Prize
in astronomy

Horsehead Nebula *is one of the best-known images in astronomy. Part of the Orion constellation, it is about 1,500 light years away.*

Nigel Sharp/NOAO/AURA/NSF

...When a faithful thinker, resolute to detach every object from personal relations, and see it in the light of thought, shall, at the same time, kindle science with the fire of the holiest affections, then will God go forth anew into the creation.

RALPH WALDO EMERSON
Nature

A common sense interpretation of the facts suggests that a super-intellect has monkeyed with physics, as well as with chemistry and biology, and that there are no blind forces worth speaking about in nature. The numbers one calculates from the facts seem to me so overwhelming as to put this conclusion almost beyond question.

SIR FRED HOYLE
British mathematician, astronomer, and cosmologist

For the scientist who has lived by his faith in the power of reason, the story ends like a bad dream. He has scaled the mountains of ignorance; he is about to conquer the highest peak; as he pulls himself over the final rock, he is greeted by a band of theologians who have been sitting there for centuries.

ROBERT JASTROW
God and the Astronomers

The Lagoon Nebula *or* **NGC 6523** *is in the constellation of Sagittarius. It glows with the red light of hydrogen excited by the radiation of very hot stars buried deep within its center. It is about 6,500 light years away and 60 light years across.*

Hubble Space Telescope/NASA/ESA

Science wants to know the mechanism of the universe, religion the meaning. The two cannot be separated. Many scientists feel there is no place in research for discussion of anything that sounds mystical. But it is unreasonable to think we already know enough about the natural world to be confident about the totality of forces.

CHARLES TOWNES
Physicist, 1964 Nobel Prize winner

Flame Nebula, NGC 2024 *(right) is estimated to be about 1,500 light years away and is part of the constellation Orion.* **Barred-spiral galaxy NGC 4314** *has clusters of infant stars that formed in a ring around the core. This stellar nursery, created within the last 5 million years, is the only place in the entire galaxy where new stars are born. NGC 4314 is one of our nearest neighbors, only 40 million light years away.*

Jason Ware

The most beautiful thing we can experience is the mysterious. It is the source of all true art and science. He to whom this emotion is a stranger, who can no longer pause to wonder and stand rapt in awe, is as good as dead: his eyes are closed.

✠   ALBERT EINSTEIN   ✠

As science explains more of the intriguing mysteries of life and the universe, its realms expand into those areas which previously were either unknown or accepted solely by faith. . . . Man is the observer of the universe, the experimenter, the searcher for truth, but he is not spectator alone. He is a participant in the continuing process of creation. He is the highest product of that creation.

WERNHER VON BRAUN
All Believers Are Brothers

Saturn's Rings—*This highly enhanced color view assembled from clear, orange, and ultraviolet frames shows variations in the chemical composition from one part of Saturn's ring system to another. Voyager 2 took these images from a distance of 5.5 million miles.*

He has made everything beautiful in its time; also he has put eternity into man's mind, yet so that he cannot find out what God has done from the beginning to the end.

ECCLESIASTES 3:11

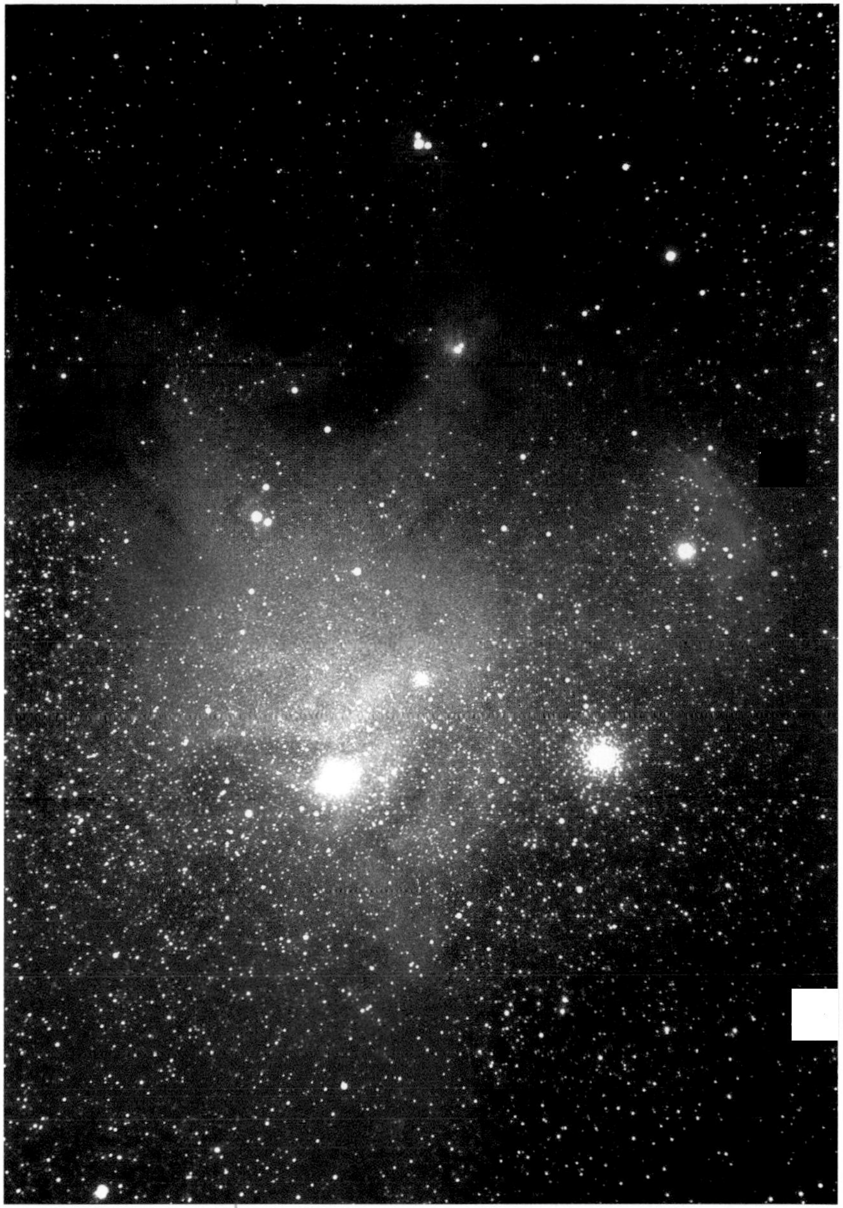

Rho Ophiuchus Nebula Complex *is one of the most beautiful areas of the night sky. It contains dark nebulae where lanes of dust hide background stars and red emission nebulae. The bright star in the center is the red giant Antares, which is about 520 light years away.*

Jerry Lodriguss

Divinity is not playful. The universe was not made in jest but in solemn incomprehensible earnest. By a power that is unfathomably secret, and holy, and fleet. There is nothing to be done about it, but ignore it, or see.

ANNIE DILLARD
Pilgrim at Tinker Creek

Stars in the Trifid Nebula—*Very hot stars, recently formed, illuminate tiny dust grains mixed in a vast cloud of hydrogen, causing the gas to glow. The stars at the heart of the nebula are associated with dust lanes, which are silhouetted against the glowing background. This nebula is in the constellation Sagittarius about 3,000 light years away.*

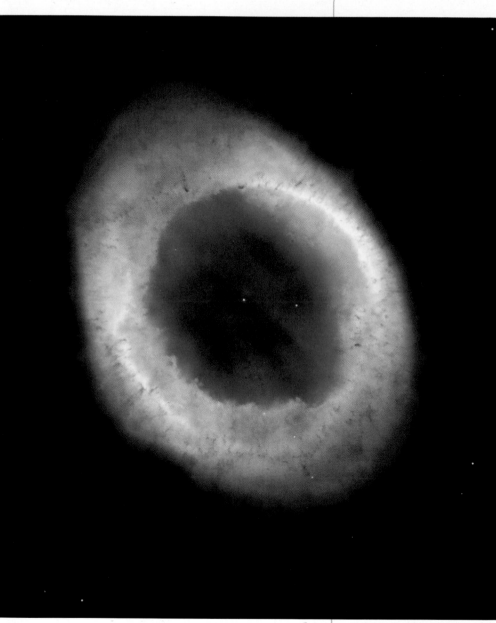

Science at the cutting edge, conducted by sharp minds probing deep into nature, is not about self-evident facts. It is about mystery and not knowing. It is about taking huge risks. It is about wasting time, getting burned, and failing. It is like trying to crack a monstrous safe that has a complicated, secret lock designed by God.

RICHARD PRESTON
First Light

Ring Nebula M57 *(left) is about 2,000 light years away and one light year in diameter. The faint speck at the center was once a star of greater mass than our sun. It is dying and ejecting its outer layers into space.*
Antennae Galaxies—*Over 1,000 bright young star clusters (blue) are bursting to life in a brief, intense, brilliant "fireworks show" at the heart of a pair of colliding galaxies.*

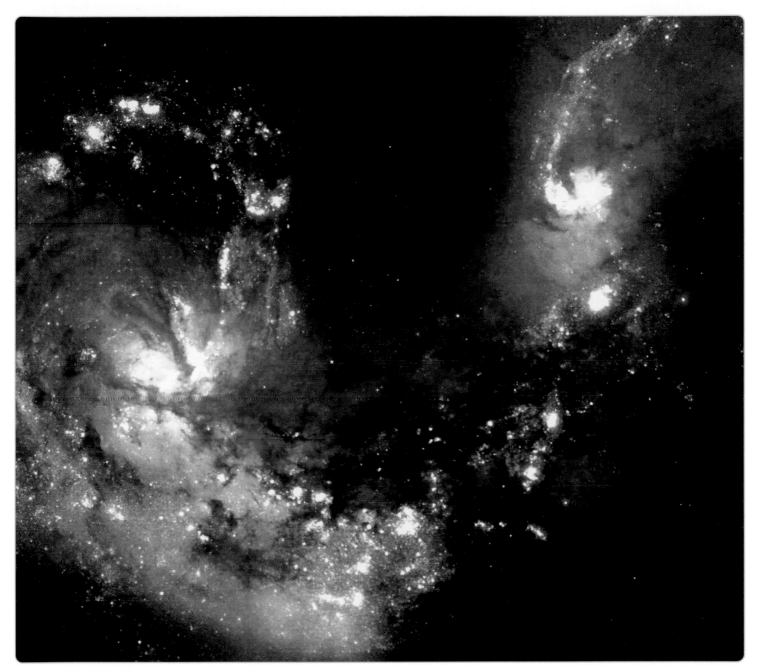

43

CISCO/Subaru/NAOJ

God does not play dice with the universe; He plays an ineffable game of his own devising, which might be compared, from the perspective of any of the other players, to being involved in an obscure and complex version of poker in a pitch dark room, with blank cards, for infinite stakes, with a dealer who won't tell you the rules, and who smiles all the time.

GAIMAN AND PRATCHETT
Good Omens

Orion Nebula—*This is an infrared image of the famous nebula located 1,500 light years away. At the center is the Trapezium, a group of four bright stars. The butterfly-like red feature at the top is the Kleinman-Low nebula.*

I still believe the universe has a beginning in real time, at a big bang. But there's another kind of time, imaginary time, at right angles to real time, in which the universe has no beginning or end. This would mean that the way the universe began would be determined by the laws of physics. One wouldn't have to say that God chose to set the universe going in some arbitrary way that we couldn't understand. It says nothing about whether or not God exists—just that He is not arbitrary.

STEPHEN HAWKING
Black Holes and Baby Universes

WR124—*This dramatic Hubble image shows an extremely rare and short-lived class of super-hot star known as a Wolf-Raynet star. It is ejecting hot clumps of gas into the surrounding nebula, M1-67, at speeds of 100,000 m.p.h. The star is 15,000 light years away in the constellation Sagittarius.*

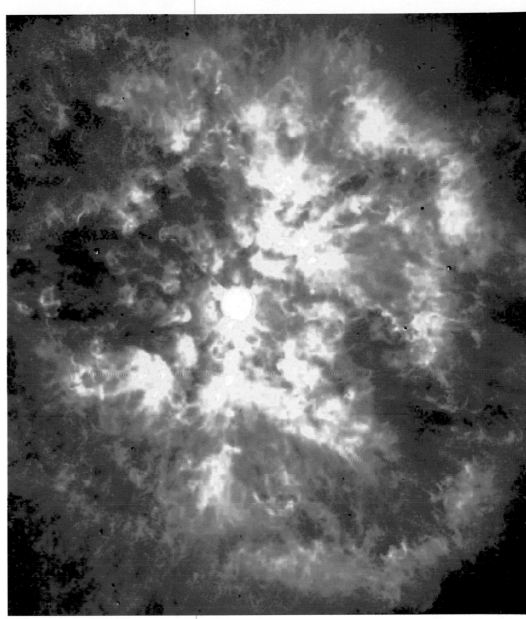

Hubble Space Telescope/NASA/ESA

45

Through our science we have created magnificent spacecrafts and telescopes to explore the night and the light and the half light. We have made visible things that are invisible to the unaided eye. We have brought the dreamy heavens down to Earth, held them in the mind's eye. Our explorations have produced a vast archive of remarkable astronomical images. . . . The riches are too many for choices, the revelations beautiful and dreadful. Who can look at these images and not be transformed? The heavens declare God's glory.

CHET RAYMO
Skeptics and True Believers

I want to know how God created this world. I am not interested in this or that phenomenon, in the spectrum of this or that element. I want to know His thoughts; the rest are details.

ALBERT EINSTEIN

30 Doradus *is located in a small neighboring galaxy called the Large Magellanic Cloud about 166,000 light years away. In the center (upper right) is a starburst region comprised of hundreds of the brightest, most massive, and most active stars known in the nearby universe.*

Jerry Lodriguss

How vast is creation! I see the planets rise and the stars hurry by, carried along with their light! What, then, is this hand which propels them?

GUSTAVE FLAUBERT
Smarh (1839)

Small Sagittarius Cloud *is a dazzling array of stars near the heart of the Milky Way, about 25,000 light years away in the constellation Sagittarius.*

The heavens speak of the Creator's glory and the sky proclaims God's handiwork.

PSALMS 19.2

For astronomy is not only pleasant, but also useful to be known; it cannot be denied that this art unfolds the admirable wisdom of God.

JOHN CALVIN
1509–1564 French theologian and reformer

Lagoon and Trifid Nebulas, *located in the Milky Way, are two of the most beautiful nebulae in the night sky. These two star-forming regions are about 6,500 and 5,000 light years away, respectively, in the constellation Sagittarius.*

Jason Ware

49

Jerry Lodriguss

The day will come when, after harnessing space, the winds, the tides and gravitation, we shall harness for God the energies of love. And on that day, for the second time in the history of the world, we shall have discovered fire.

⊹   PIERRE TEILHARD DE CHARDIN   ⊹

The Pleiades *is a relatively nearby open cluster of stars, about 370 light years away. The cluster is surrounded by blue nebulosity illuminated by nearby stars. Often mistaken for the Little Dipper, it is in the constellation Taurus.*

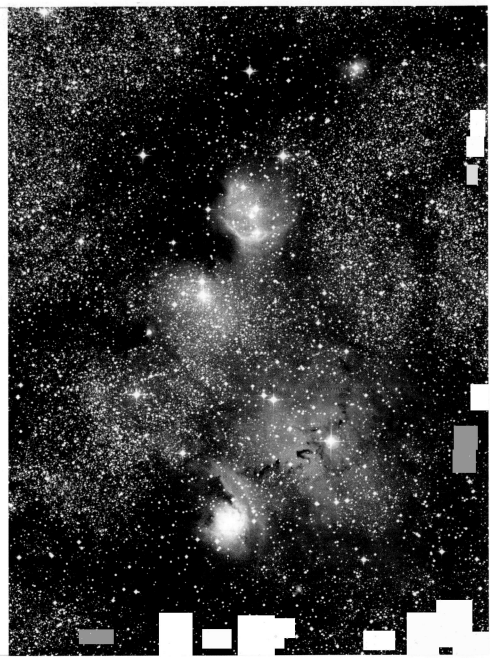

With all your science can you tell how it is, and whence it is, that light comes into the soul?

Henry David Thoreau

I have . . . a terrible need . . . shall I say the word? . . . of religion. Then I go out at night and paint the stars.

Vincent Van Gogh

NGC 6559 and **IC 1274-75** *in Sagittarius This dusty region is associated with the brighter and better known Trifid and Lagoon Nebulae, which are nearby. The soft reddish glow of fluorescent hydrogen is evidence that there are hot young stars associated with the dusty clouds.*

H e saw God's foot upon the treadle of the loom, and spoke it; and thereafter his shipmates called him mad. So man's insanity is heaven's sense.

HERMAN MELVILLE
Moby Dick

Dark Cloud in Scorpius—*This curious massive dark nebula is as yet unnamed. Its swept-back shape is governed by radiation from very luminous stars some distance from the nebula. The source of energy is the Scorpius OB association, a group of brilliant, very hot stars, about 5,000 light years away.*

This new knowledge of the galaxies is exhilarating and terrifying, beautiful and dreadful....The Hubble Deep Field photo opens us to a cosmos of capacious grandeur—a universe of 50 billion galaxies blowing like snowflakes in a cosmic storm. . . .The fourteenth-century mystic Julian of Norwich asked, "What is the use of praying if God does not answer?" In that wonderful image of more than 1,000 galaxies caught by a magnificent instrument lofted into space by a questioning creature, God answers.

CHET RAYMO
Skeptics and True Believers

Galaxies Across Billions of Years—*Mankind's deepest, most detailed optical view of the universe. Representing a narrow keyhole view stretching to the visible horizon of the universe, this Hubble Deep Field image covers a speck of the sky only about the width of a dime located 75 feet away. Within this small field, considered representative of the distribution of galaxies throughout the universe, are a bewildering assortment of at least 1,500 galaxies in various stages of development. Some of the galaxies probably date back to the beginning of the universe, 12 to 13 billion years ago.*

I had an experience I can't prove, I can't even explain it, but everything that I know as a human being, everything that I am tells me that it was real. I was part of something wonderful, something that changed me forever; a vision of the Universe that tells us undeniably how tiny, and insignificant, and how rare and precious we all are. A vision that tells us we belong to something that is greater than ourselves. That we are not, that none of us, are alone.

CARL SAGAN
Ellie Arroway, *Contact*

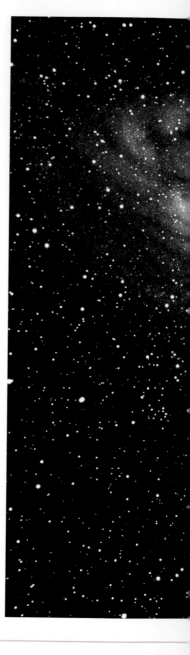

Andromeda Galaxy M31 *is a large spiral galaxy very similar in appearance to our own galaxy and our closest neighbor. A gigantic collection of more than 300 billion stars, it is about 65,000 light years across and about 2.93 million light years away.*

Jason Ware

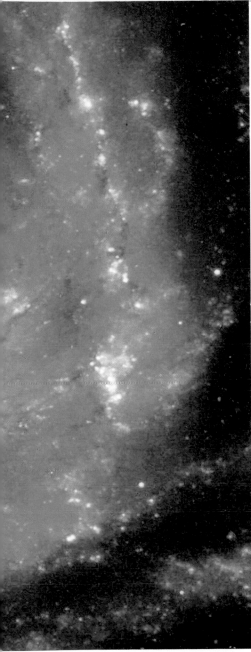

I belong to the group of scientists who do not subscribe to a conventional religion but nevertheless deny that the universe is a purposeless accident. Through my scientific work I have come to believe more and more strongly that the physical universe is put together with an ingenuity so astonishing that I cannot accept it merely as a brute fact. There must, it seems to me, be a deeper level of explanation. Whether one wishes to call that deeper level "God" is a matter of taste and definition.

PAUL DAVIES
The Mind of God

Spiral Galaxy NGC 1232 *is about twice the size of the Milky Way, 200,000 light years across. Millions of bright stars and dark dust are caught up in the gravitational pull of the spiral arms rotating about the center. Open clusters with bright blue young stars are visible along the arms. Less visible, but detectable, are hundreds of billions of dim normal stars, and vast tracts of inter-stellar gas, together containing so much mass that they dominate the dynamics of the inner galaxy. NGC 1232 is about 100 million light years away in the constellation Eridanus (The River).*

Jean-Charles Cullandre/CFHT

It could be that God has not absconded but spread, as our vision and understanding of the universe have spread, to a fabric of spirit and sense so grand and subtle, so powerful in a new way, that we can only feel blindly of its hem.

ANNIE DILLARD
Pilgrim at Tinker Creek

The Sombrero NGC 4594—*Named after the broad-brimmed Mexican hat it resembles, the Sombrero is probably the most famous galaxy in the sky. The light from this spiral system is dominated by billions of old faint stars that form the huge bulge around its small hidden nucleus. Some astronomers speculate that a black hole lies at the center of the Sombrero, which is 50 million light years away.*

Southern Band of the Milky Way *(next page) as seen from Australia. Visible are many bright stars, dark dust lanes, red emission nebulae, blue reflection nebulae, and clusters of stars.*

Behind it all is surely an idea so simple, so beautiful, so compelling that
when—in a decade, a century, or a millennium—we grasp it,
we will say to each other, how could it have been otherwise?
How could we have been so blind for so long?

✢ JOHN ARCHIBALD WHEELER ✢

John P. Gleason

But I don't have to know an answer. I don't feel frightened by not knowing things,
by being lost in the mysterious universe without having any purpose,
which is the way it really is, as far as I can tell, possibly.
It doesn't frighten me.

RICHARD FEYNMAN
For the Pleasure of Finding Things Out

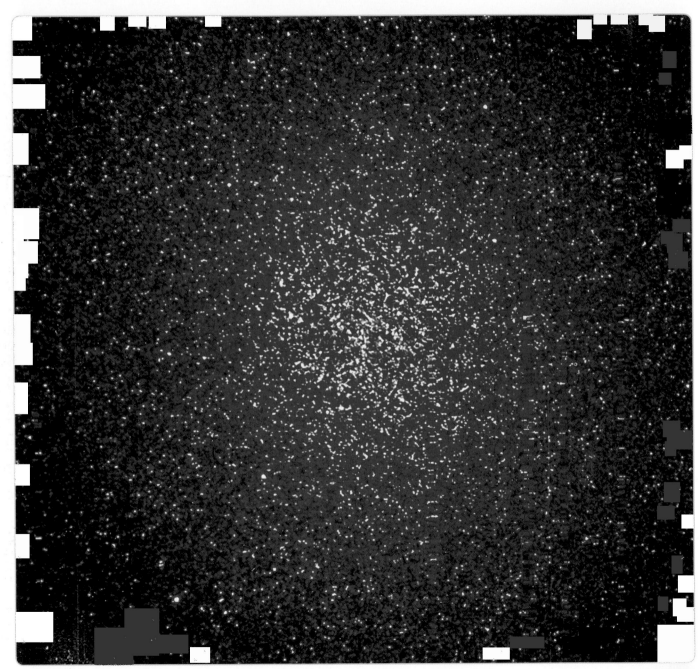

There are more things in heaven and Earth, Horatio, than are dreamt of in your philosophy.

WILLIAM SHAKESPEARE
Hamlet

Omega Centauri *(left) is a giant globular star cluster which is well known to observers of the southern sky. It is relatively close (17,000 light years) and immense (150 light years across) and contains more than one million stars.*
Sagittarius Star Cloud SGR-I *(right) is a narrow, dust-free region of the Milky Way that contains some of the oldest inhabitants of our galaxy. Most of the stars are orange or red like our sun; the bluish green are young, massive, and very hot. The bright red stars are older, cooler, red giants. It is about 25,000 light years away.*

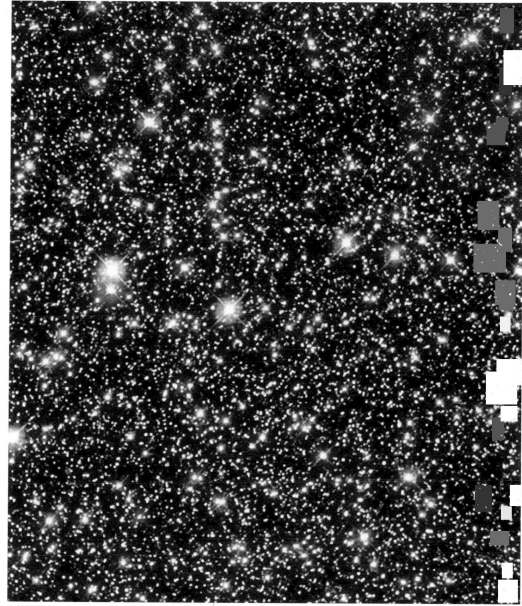

Hubble Heritage Team/AURA/STScI/NASA

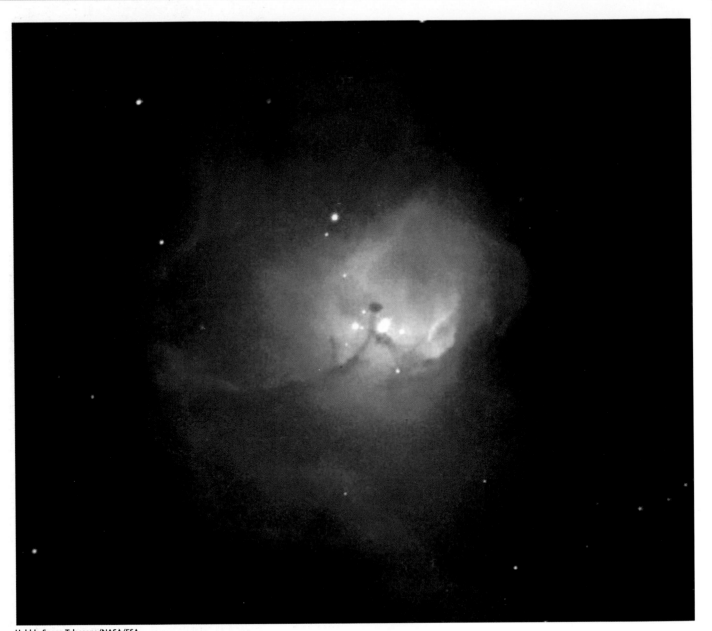

Hubble Space Telescope/NASA/ESA

◈ Instead of an intellectual search, there was suddenly a very deep gut feeling that something was different . . . seeing that Sun . . . set in the background of the very deep black and velvety cosmos, seeing—rather, knowing for sure—that there was a purposefulness of flow, of energy, of time, of space in the cosmos—that it was beyond man's rational ability to understand, that suddenly there was a nonrational way of understanding that had been beyond my previous experience. . . . On the return trip home, gazing through 240,000 miles of space toward the stars and the planet from which I had come, I suddenly experienced the universe as intelligent, loving, harmonious.

EDGAR MITCHELL
U.S. Astronaut

Massive Star Cluster N81 *(left) is a group of young, ultrabright stars nested in their embryonic cloud of glowing gases, located 200,000 light years away in the Small Magellanic Cloud. This is a close-up glimpse of the firestorm accompanying the birth of extremely massive stars, each blazing with the brilliance of 300,000 of our suns.*
Earthrise *(right) as seen from the moon.*

Apollo 11/NASA

Stars are like animals in the wild.
We may see the young but never the actual birth,
which is a veiled and secret event.

✛ HEINZ PAGELS ✛
Perfect Symmetry

Star Birth Region NGC 604 *lies in a spiral arm of the galaxy M33, and is a close neighbor to our own Milky Way, only 2.7 million light years away. This vast star-forming region is about 1,500 light years across.*

Hubble Space Telescope/NASA/ESA

Because a star explodes and a thousand worlds like ours die,
we know this world is.
That is the smile: that what might not be, is.

JOHN FOWLES
The Magus

Doomed Star Eta Carinae *has a mass approximately 150 times greater than our sun and is about 4 million times brighter. It is over 10,000 light years away and prone to violent outbursts. The rapidly expanding shell was ejected from its last outburst in 1841, and is moving outward at more than 2 million miles per hour. The star is one of stellar astronomy's great mysteries.*

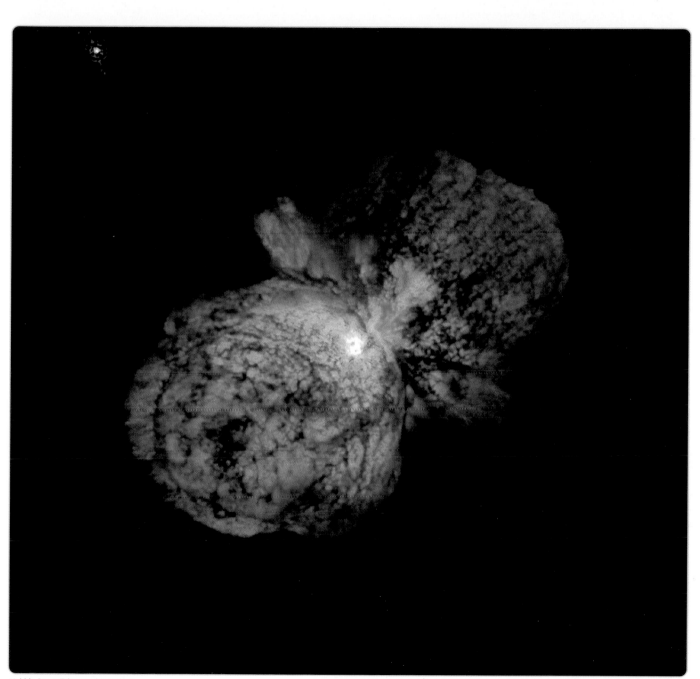

Hubble Space Telescope/NASA/ESA

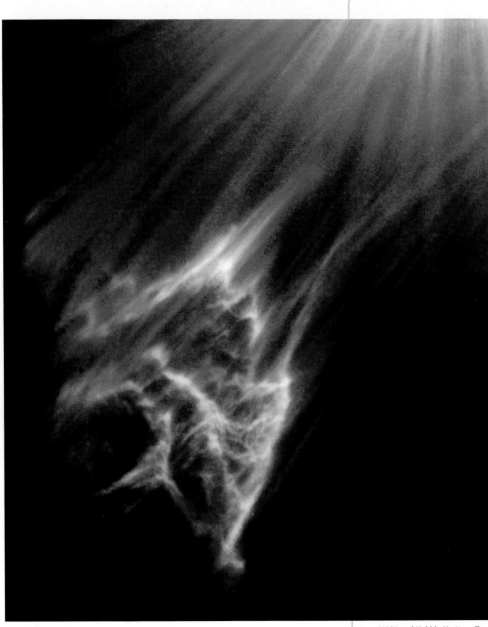

NASA and Hubble Heritage Team

W hat is it that breathes fire into the equations and makes a universe for them to govern? . . . Although science may solve the problem of how the universe began, it cannot answer the question: Why does the universe bother to exist? I don't know the answer to that.

STEPHEN HAWKING
Black Holes and Baby Universes

Pleiades Reflection Nebula IC 349—*The wispy tendrils of a dark interstellar cloud are being destroyed by the passage of one of the brightest stars in the Pleiades star cluster. The star is reflecting light off the surface of pitch black clouds of cold gas laced with dust. This chance collision allows astronomers to study interstellar material under very rare conditions. The Pleiades Nebula is in the constellation Taurus about 380 light years from earth.*

Chandra X-ray Observatory/ACIS

Radio Galaxy Pictor A—*This x-ray image shows a spectacular jet that emanates from the center of the galaxy (left) and extends across 360,000 light years towards a brilliant hot spot. The hot spot is at least 800,000 light years away from where the jet originates. The jet is thought to be produced by powerful electromagnetic forces created by a black hole. While most material falls into a black hole, some can be ejected at extremely high speeds.*

The highest happiness of man . . . is to have probed what is knowable and quietly to revere what is unknowable.

JOHANN WOLFGANG VON GOETHE

More appropriate, I should think, is the view that God created the universe out of an interest in spontaneous creativity—that he wanted nature to produce surprises, phenomena that he himself could not have foreseen. What would such a creative universe be like? Well, it would for one thing be impossible to predict in detail. And this seems to be the case with the universe we inhabit.... Further, a creative universe should give rise to agencies that are themselves creative, which is to say unpredictable. There is in our universe such an agency, spectacularly successful at reversing the dreary slide of entropy and making surprising things happen.
We call it life.

TIMOTHY FERRIS
The Whole Shebang

The Bubble Nebula NGC 7635 *is an expanding shell of gas surrounding a hot, massive star in the Milky Way. The star which is 40 times larger than our sun, is responsible for a stellar wind moving at 4 million miles per hour, which propels particles off the surface of the star. The fingers at the top of the image are dense clumps of molecular gas which have not yet encountered the expanding shell. The bubble is about 10 light years across and 11,300 light years away in the constellation Cassiopeia.*

75

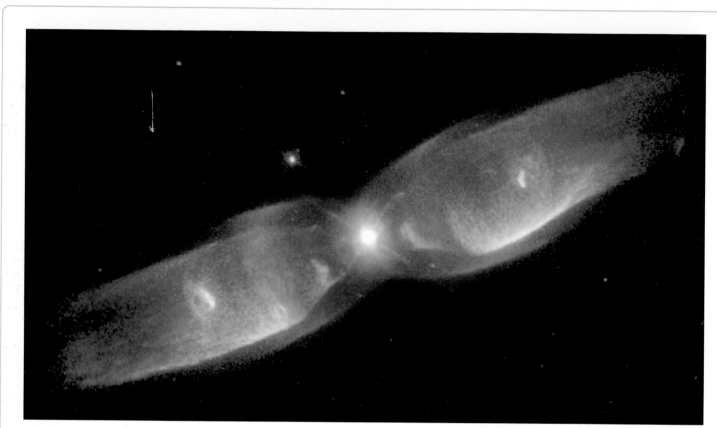

For after all what is man in nature? A nothing in relation to infinity, all in relation to nothing,
a central point between nothing and all and infinitely far from understanding either.
The ends of things and their beginnings are impregnably concealed from him in
an impenetrable secret. He is equally incapable of seeing the nothingness out
of which he was drawn and the infinite in which he is engulfed.

BLAISE PASCAL
Pensées

Depend upon it, it is not the want of greater miracles, but of the soul to perceive such as are allowed us still, that makes us push all the sanctities into the far spaces we cannot reach.

JAMES MARTINEAU
sermon, "Help Thou Mine Unbelief "

Butterfly Nebula M2-9 *(left) is a bipolar planetary nebula. Gases ejected from a pair of central stars, moving in excess of 200 miles per second, give the appearance of a supersonic jet exhaust. The high-speed wind from one of the stars as it rams into the surrounding disk serves as a nozzle: the wind is then deflected and forms the pair of jets seen in the image. M2-9 is 2,100 light years away in the constellation Ophiuchus.*

Orion Nebula NGC 1976 *(right) — This spectacular nebula was first noted as an extended nebula in 1610, only a year after Galileo's first use of the telescope. This star-forming region is very young by astronomical standards, about 30,000 years old. Stars are being born in a dense cloud behind the nebula, which is about 1,600 light years away in the constellation Orion.*

Oh, I have slipped the surly bonds of earth
And danced the skies on laughter-silvered wings;
Sunward I've climbed, and joined the tumbling mirth
Of sun-split clouds, and done a hundred things
You have not dreamed of, wheeled and soared and swung
High in the sunlit silence. Hov'ring there,
I've chased the shouting wind along, and flung
My eager craft through footless halls of air.
Up, up the long, delirious, burning blue
I've topped the windswept heights with easy grace
Where never lark, or even eagle flew
And, while with silent, lifting mind I've trod
The high untrespassed sanctity of space,
Put out my hand, and touched the face of God.

"HIGH FLIGHT," BY JOHN GILLESPIE MAGEE, JR.
killed in the Battle of Britain, age 19

Eagle Nebula—*This detail of the famous emission nebula shows the denser star-forming knots. Energetic light from young massive stars causes the gas to glow and boils away part of the dust and gas from its birth pillar. Many of these stars will explode after several million years, returning most of their elements back to the nebula that formed them. This process is forming an open cluster of stars known as M16, which can be partially seen in the upper right. The Eagle Nebula is about 7,000 light years away in the constellation Serpens.*

The physicists are getting things down to the nitty-gritty, they've really just about pared things down to the ultimate details, and the last thing they ever expected to happen is happening. God is showing through....They've been scraping away at physical reality all these centuries, and now the layer of the little left we don't understand is so fine, God's face is staring right out at us.

JOHN UPDIKE
Roger's Version

The God of my early religious training pulled off tricks that are not beyond the powers of any competent conjuror; Harry Houdini or David Copperfield could turn a stick into a serpent or water into wine without batting an eye. But no Houdini or Copperfield can turn microscopic cells into a flock of birds and send them flying on their planet-spinning course. No Houdini or Copperfield can cause consciousness to flare out and embrace the eons and the galaxies.

CHET RAYMO
Skeptics and True Believers

Hodge 301 *(seen at the lower right of the image) is a cluster of brilliant, massive stars in the center of the most violent starburst region in the local universe. It is located in the Tarantula Nebula, which is part of our nearest galactic neighbor, the Large Magellanic Cloud. Many of the stars in Hodge 301 are so old they have exploded as supernovas and are blasting material out at speeds of almost 300 miles per second, shocking and pressing the gas into a multitude of sheets and filaments.*

Hubble Space Telescope/NASA/ESA

As you do not know how the spirit comes to the bones in the womb of a woman with child, so you do not know the work of God who makes everything.

ECCLESIASTES 11.5

Helix Nebula *(left)—This image shows the collision of two gases near a dying star. Astronomers have dubbed the tadpolelike objects "cometary knots." Each gaseous head is at least twice the size of our solar system and each tail stretches 100 billion miles. The Helix Nebula is 450 light years away and part of the constellation Aquarius.*
Starbirth in Orion *(right)—A churning, turbulent star factory set within a maelstrom of flowing luminescent gas, illuminated by a torrent of energetic ultraviolet light from its four hottest and most massive stars (center left), known as the Trapezium. This stellar cavern also contains hundreds of other young stars at various stages of formation, and more than one hundred protoplanetary disks that are believed to be embryonic solar systems that will eventually form planets.*

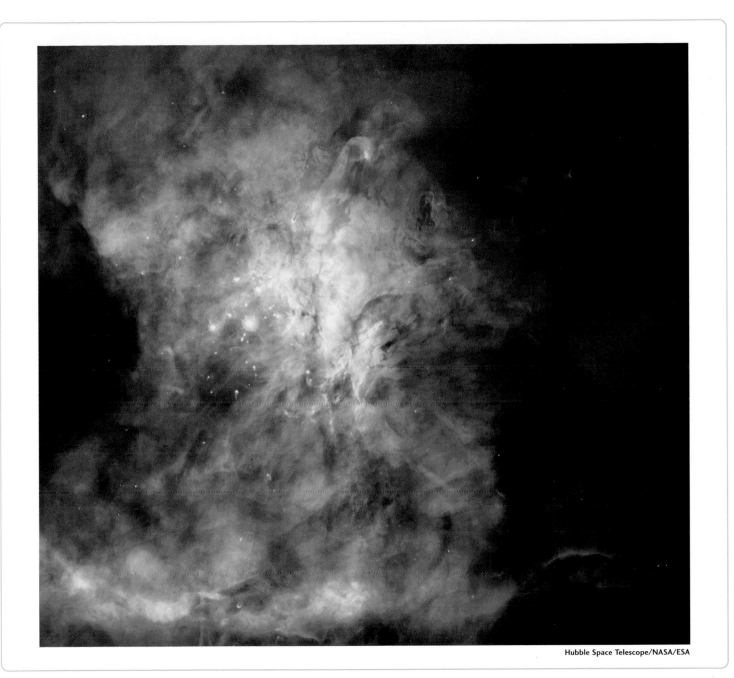

Hubble Space Telescope/NASA/ESA

My theology, briefly, is that the universe was dictated but not signed.

⊹ CHRISTOPHER MORLEY

I do not feel obliged to believe that the same God who has endowed us with sense, reason, and intellect has intended us to forgo their use.

⊹ GALILEO

Hickson Compact Group 87 *is a group of four galaxies about 400 million years away in the constellation Capricorn. The disk-shaped galaxy in the front (HGC87a) and its nearby neighbor (87b) to the right, are thought to harbor black holes at their center.*

God said to Abraham, "But for me, you would not be here." "I know that, Lord," Abraham answered, "but were I not here, there would be no one to think about you."

✣ TRADITIONAL JEWISH TALE

Polar-ring Galaxy NGC 4650A, *located about 130 million light years away, is one of only 100 known polar-ring galaxies. This unusual disk-ring structure is not fully understood. One possibility is that the rings are the remnants of colossal collisions between two galaxies at least 1 billion years ago.*

B lack holes would seem to suggest that God not only plays dice
but also sometimes throws them where they cannot be seen.

STEPHEN HAWKING
Black Holes and Baby Universes

Black Hole Feeding—*A massive black hole hidden at the center of a nearby giant galaxy, Centaurus A, is feeding on a smaller galaxy in a spectacular collision. Such fireworks were common in the early universe, as galaxies formed and evolved, but are rare today. Centaurus A is located 10 million light years away and contains the closest active galactic nucleus to Earth.*

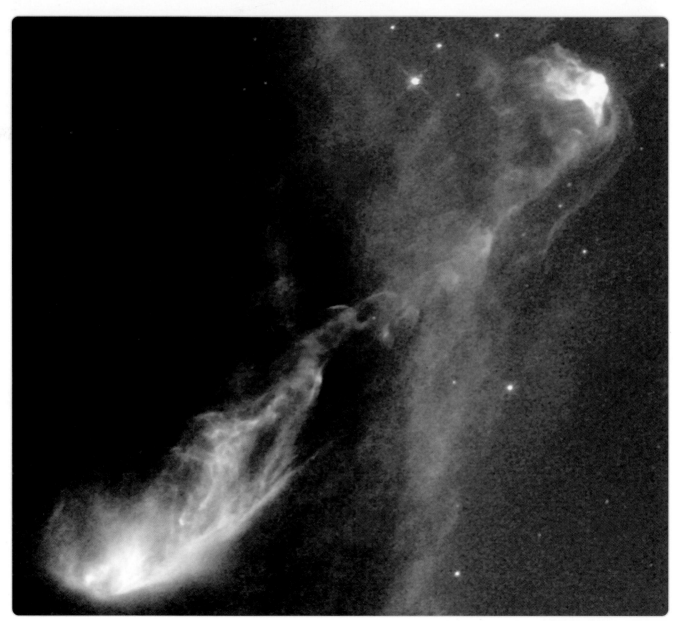

Hubble Space Telescope/NASA/ESA

It is the sense of mystery that, in my opinion, drives the true scientist; the same blind force, blindly seeing, deafly hearing, unconsciously remembering, that drives the larva into the butterfly. If [the scientist] has not experienced, at least a few times in his life, this cold shudder down his spine, this confrontation with an immense invisible face whose breath moves him to tears, he is not a scientist.

ERWIN CHARGAFF
Biologist

It is the nature of God to reside in mystery—ineluctable, inexhaustible mystery. We do not need to understand the cabala of mathematical physics to apprehend the *mysterium tremendum*. We need only look out the window.

CHET RAYMO
Skeptics and True Believers

Stellar Jets *from the birth of a new star are a trillion miles long. This is one of the first close-up images of the dynamic process accompanying the final stages of a star's birth. The jet called HH-47 reveals a complicated pattern that indicates that the star which is hidden inside the dust cloud might be wobbling. It is 1,500 light years away in the constellation Vela.*

After close on two centuries of passionate struggles, neither science nor faith has succeeded in discrediting its adversary. On the contrary, it becomes obvious that neither can develop normally without the other. And the reason is simple: the same life animates both. Neither in its impetus nor its achievements can science go to its limits without becoming tinged with mysticism and charged with faith.

PIERRE TEILHARD DE CHARDIN
The Phenomenon of Man

Star Formation in Ara—*Red-glowing hydrogen gas, hot blue stars, and dark obscuring dust clouds are scattered throughout this dramatic region of the Milky Way in the southern constellation of Ara (the Alter), which is about 4,000 light years away. Visible within the dark dust nebula in the bottom center is a small cluster of newborn stars.*

VLT/European Southern Observatory

The important thing is not to stop questioning.
Curiosity has its own reason for existing.
One cannot help but be in awe when he contemplates
the mysteries of eternity, of life, of the marvelous structure of reality.
It is enough if one tries merely to comprehend
a little of this mystery every day.

✢ ALBERT EINSTEIN ✢

Spiral Galaxy NGC 1232—*This computer processed (U-B color-index image) shows the differences between images of the galaxy as seen in different wavebands. Star formation regions that emit strong ultraviolet light therefore appear very bright. NGC 1232 is in the constellation Eridanus and has a diameter of nearly 200,000 light years, about twice the size of the Milky Way. It is about 100 million light years from Earth.*

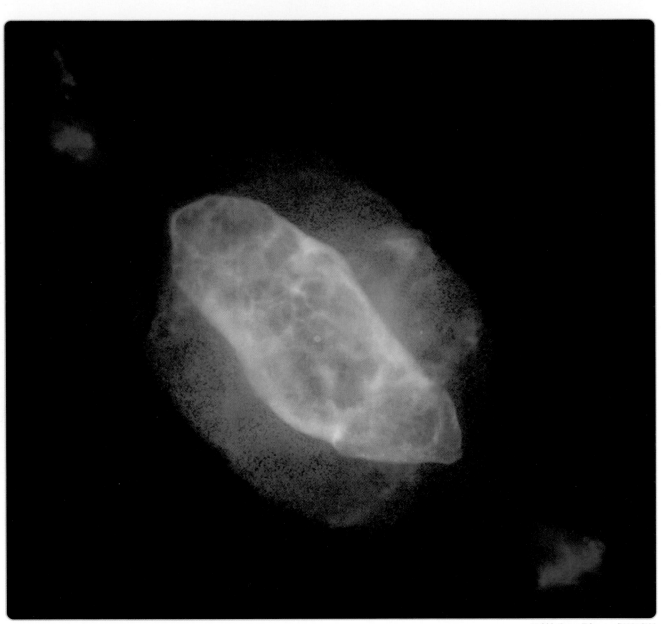

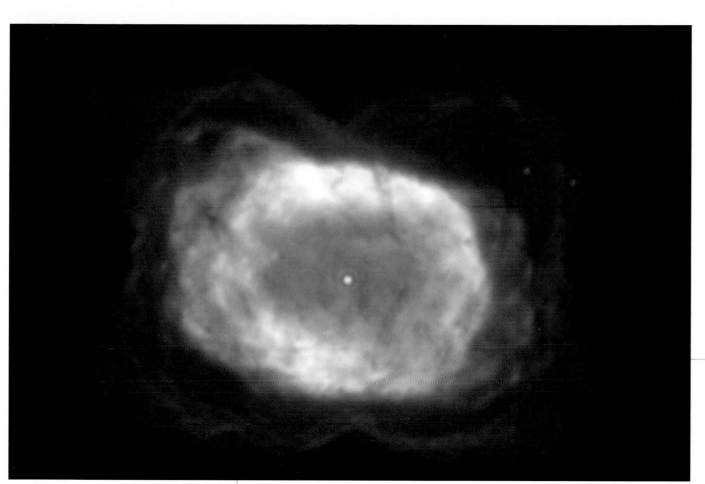

Planetary Nebula—*Both images are stages in the spectacular death of medium mass stars like our sun. A star can become a planetary nebula after it depletes its nuclear fuel and begins puffing away layers of material. The material settles into a wind of gas and dust blowing away from the dying star, and intense ultraviolet radiation from the central star lights up a region of the surrounding gas. Someday our own sun will have a similar colorful ending, burning Earth to a cinder in the process.*

The forms and creeds of religion change, but the sentiment of religion—the wonder and reverence and love we feel in the presence of the inscrutable universe—persists.

JOHN BURROUGHS
Time and Change

Who blew the Bellows of his Furnace Vast
Or held the Mould wherein the world was Cast?

⊹   EDWARD TAYLOR   ⊹
The Preface

Ant Nebula MZ3 *(above)—The ejection of gas from the dying star at the center has a very unusual symmetrical pattern, which scientists do not yet understand.*

The Sun *(right)—Our solar system's star, provider of heat and light to our planet. This image shows many prominences and active regions.*

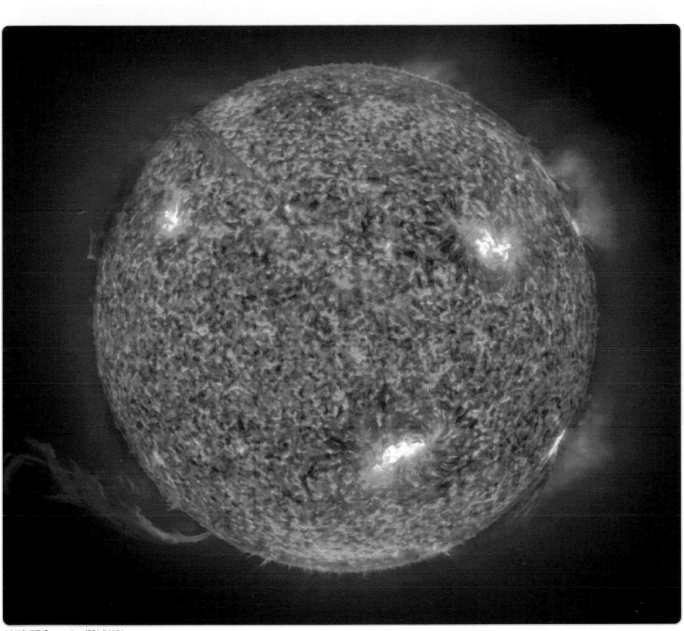

SOHO-EIT Consortium/ESA/NASA

The Moon

Galileo/JPL/NASA

Earth

The final mystery is oneself. When one has weighed the sun in the balance, and measured the steps of the moon, and mapped out the seven heavens star by star, there still remains oneself. Who can calculate the orbit of his own soul?

OSCAR WILDE
De Profundis

Spiral Galaxy NGC 4414—*As a result of careful brightness measurements of variable stars, astronomers have been able to measure the precise distance to this massive galaxy. It is 19.1 megaparsecs or about 60 million light years away. The central regions of this galaxy, as is typical of most spirals, contain primarily older yellow and red stars. The outer spiral arms are bluer due to ongoing formation of young, blue stars. The arms are also rich clouds of interstellar dust, seen as dark patches and streaks.*

Hubble Heritage Team/AURA/STScI/NASA

Once we see, however, that the probability of life originating at random is so utterly minuscule as to make it absurd, it becomes sensible to think that the favorable properties of physics on which life depends are in every respect deliberate. . . It is therefore almost inevitable that our own measure of intelligence must reflect . . . higher intelligences . . . even to the limit of God . . . .

SIR FRED HOYLE
British mathematician, astronomer, and cosmologist

. . .Every common biological organism is more intricately articulated, more astoundingly put together, than the most sublime literary composition . . . Despite all evasions, the ultimate agency of intelligence stares one in the face.

FREDERICK FERRE
Basic Modern Philosophy of Religion

Star Formation Fireworks Light up a Galaxy—*Located about 13 million light years from Earth NGC 4214 is currently forming clusters of new stars from its interstellar gas and dust. The youngest of these clusters are located at the lower right of the image, appearing as about a half dozen bright clumps of glowing gas. Near the center is a cluster of hundreds of massive blue stars, each more than 10,000 times brighter than our Sun. A vast bubble, inflated by the combined stellar winds and radiation pressure, surrounds the cluster. This bubble will continue to expand as the most massive stars in the center reach the end of their lives and explode as supernovae.*

Hubble Heritage Team/AURA/STScI/NASA

Hubble Heritage Team/AURA/STScI/NASA

God does not think; he creates.
He does not exist; he is eternal.

☩　SØREN KIERKEGAARD　☩

NGC 3603—*This image of the giant galactic nebula shows the various stages in the life cycle of stars in a single view. To the upper right is the evolved supergiant called Sher 25, which has a unique glowing ring and is flanked by ejected blobs of gas. Below Sher 25 is a starburst cluster dominated by young, hot Wolf-Rayet stars. The giant pillars of glowing hydrogen signal newborn stars emerging from their dense, gaseous nurseries.*

There is for me powerful evidence that there is something going on behind it all.... It seems as though somebody has fine-tuned nature's numbers to make the Universe.... The impression of design is overwhelming.

PAUL DAVIES
The Cosmic Blueprint

Science conducts us, step by step, through the whole range of creation, until we arrive, at length, at God.

MARGUERITE DE VALOIS
Memoirs

Supernova Remnant EO102-72 *is the remnant of a star that exploded in a nearby galaxy (Small Magellanic Cloud) about 189,000 years ago. This image is a composite of three different photographs in three different types of light. Radio waves (red) show the shock waves expanding out from the detonated star. Optical light (green) traces clumps of relatively cool oxygen, and x-rays (blue) show the relatively hot gases. EO102-72 is 40 million light years across.*

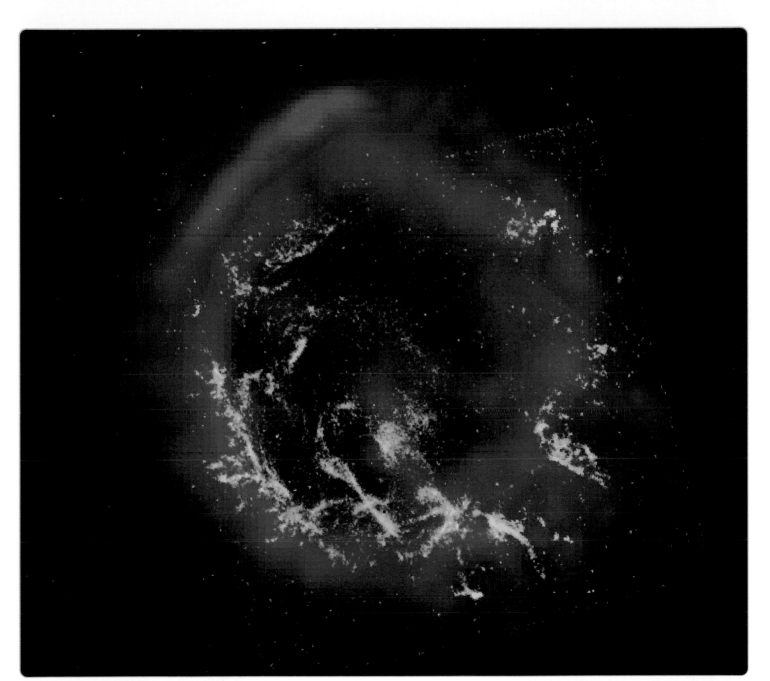

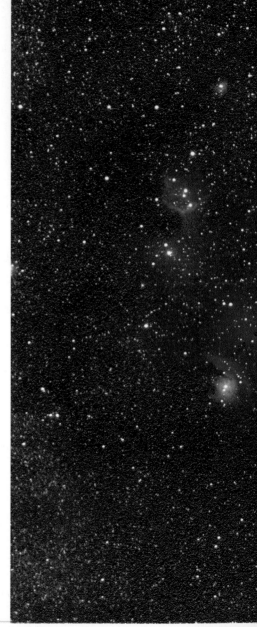

I believe in one God—sole, eternal—He who, motionless,
moves all the heavens with his love and his desire . . .
This is the origin, this is the spark that then extends into
a vivid flame and, like a star in heaven, glows in me.

DANTE ALIGHIERI
Paradiso XXIV

Lagoon Nebula *is 5,000 light years away, and home to many young stars and hot, luminous hydrogen gas. The Lagoon is so large and bright it can be seen without a telescope. Sprinkled throughout the nebula are dark clouds or Bok globules, which are a very early stage of star formation.*

John P. Gleason

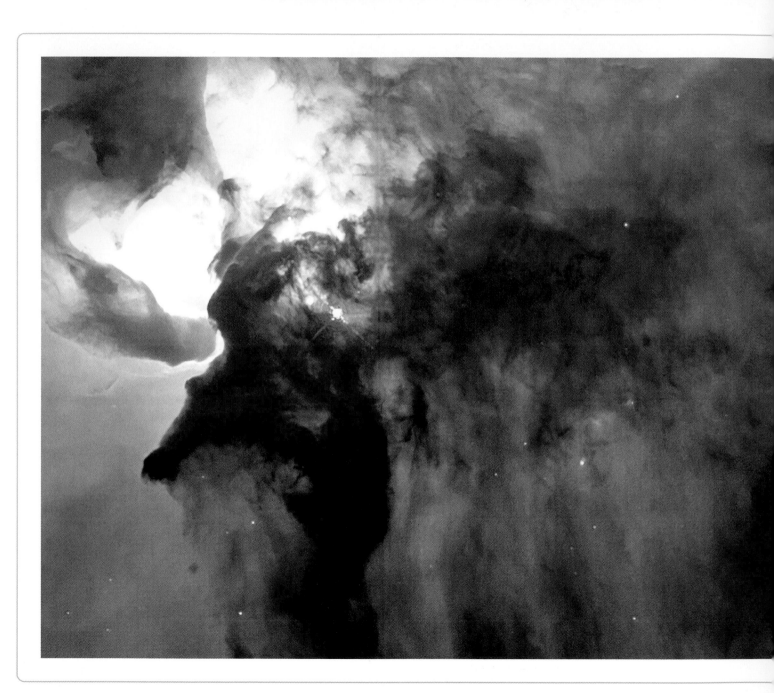

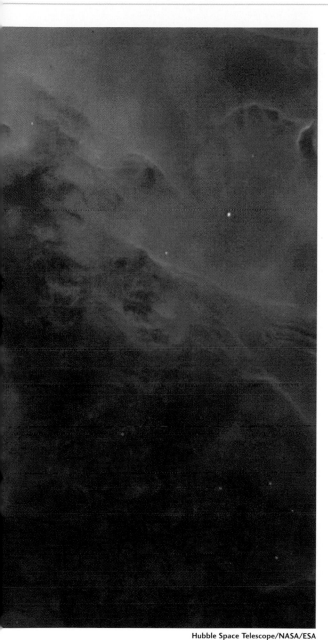

The question from agnosticism is,
Who turned on the lights?
The question from faith is,
Whatever for?

ANNIE DILLARD
Pilgrim at Tinker Creek

Lagoon Nebula NGC 6523—*A pair of interstellar "twisters"—funnels and twisted-rope structures—inhabit the brilliant "Hourglass" heart of the Lagoon Nebula, which lies 5,000 light years away towards the constellation Sagittarius. The twisters are created much the way tornadoes are produced on Earth, by a strong horizontal "shear" caused by the large difference in temperature between the hot surface and cold interior of the clouds. The central star, Herschel 36 (middle left), is the primary source of radiation for the brightest region of the nebula, called the Hourglass.*

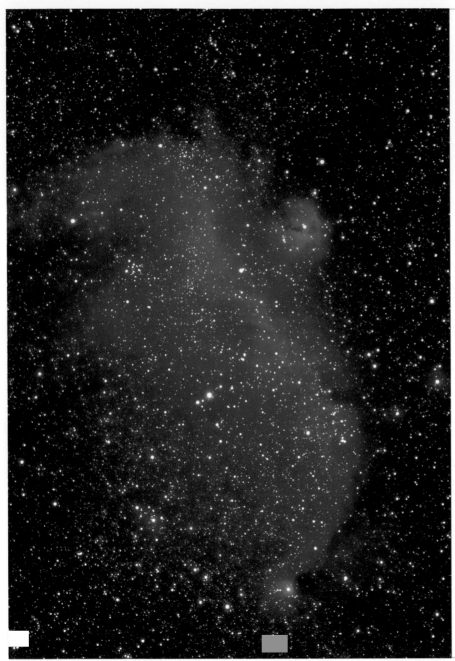

Astronomy leads us to a unique event, a universe which was created out of nothing, one with the very delicate balance needed to provide exactly the conditions required to permit life, and one which has an underlying (one might say "supernatural") plan.

ARNO PENZIAS
Nobel prizewinner in physics

Seagull Nebula IC 2177—*A large nebula straddling the border of the constellations Canis Major and Monoceros. The Seagull Nebula is many trillions of miles across, containing enough hydrogen to give rise to hundreds of stars like our sun. These then radiate the energy that irradiates the gas in the nebula and causes it to glow. The bright star at the lower "wingtip" marks Cederblad 90, a small but prominent emission nebula with an adjacent dark nebula region, visible as a region of few stars immediately to the right of the bright lower "wingtip."*

Jerry Lodriguss

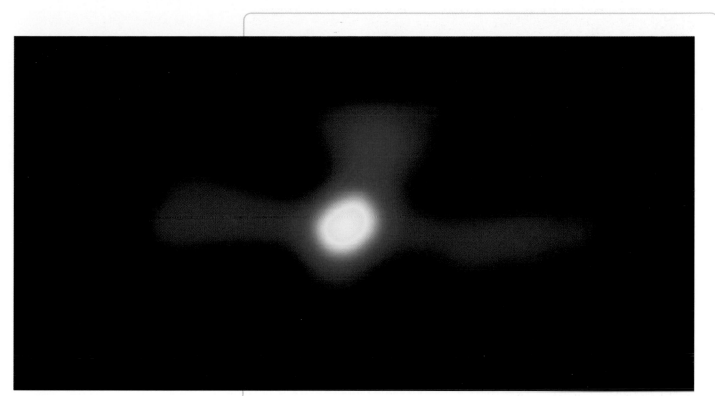

CGRO/NASA

Cloud of Antimatter—*The Compton Gamma Ray Observatory detected this new and unexpected cloud of antimatter near the center of the Milky Way Galaxy, the origin of which is a mystery. It could have been caused by the explosions of young massive stars, jets of material from a black hole in the center of the galaxy, the merger of two neutron stars or some new, unknown source. Evidence points to the existence of a huge black hole with the mass of a million suns at the center of our galaxy. Gamma rays, which have 250,000 times the energy of normal light, are produced when antimatter (positrons) and matter (electrons) collide and annihilate, converting all their mass to energy according to Einstein's famous equation $E=mc^2$.*

As we survey all the evidence, the thought insistently arises that some supernatural agency—or, rather, Agency—must be involved. Is it possible that suddenly, without intending to, we have stumbled upon scientific proof of the existence of a Supreme Being? Was it God who stepped in and so providentially crafted the cosmos for our benefit?

GEORGE GREENSTEIN
The Symbiotic Universe

Yet who seeing the snowflake, who seeing simple lipid molecules cast adrift in water forming themselves into cell-like hollow lipid vesicles, who seeing the potential for the crystallization of life in swarms of reacting molecules, who seeing the stunning order for free in networks linking tens upon tens of thousands of variables, can fail to entertain a central thought: if ever we are to attain a final theory in biology, we will surely . . . have to see that we are the natural expressions of a deeper order. Ultimately, we will discover in our creation myth that we are expected after all.

STUART KAUFFMAN
At Home in the Universe

Pipe Dark Nebula LDN 1773—*So-called because of its resemblance to the smoke from a pipe, the Pipe Nebula is part of a larger complex of dark nebulae located about a third of the way from the Lagoon Nebula to Antares, where the Pipe appears as the hind quarters of a galactic "horse," visible here at the lower left of the photo. The dark clouds are caused by absorption of background starlight by dust. To the right is a large complex of red emission nebulae and blue reflection nebulae near Antares and Rho Ophiuchus.*

Jerry Lodriguss

Whether heaven move or earth
Imports not, if thou reckon right; the rest
From man and angel the great Architect
Did wisely to conceal and not divulge
His secrets to be scanned by them who ought
Rather admire.

⊹ JOHN MILTON ⊹
Paradise Lost

Molecular Cloud Barnard 86—*What appears here as a hole in the sky is now known to astronomers as a dark molecular cloud or dark absorption nebulae. The high concentration of dust and molecular gas absorbs almost all the visible light emitted from background stars, causing black voids of varying shapes. One of the most notable of these dark absorption nebula is Barnard 68, a cloud located toward the constellation Ophiuchus, about 500 light years away and half a light year across. Very possibly the birthplace of new stars, molecular clouds develop mysteriously and are considered to be some of the coldest and most isolated places in the universe.*

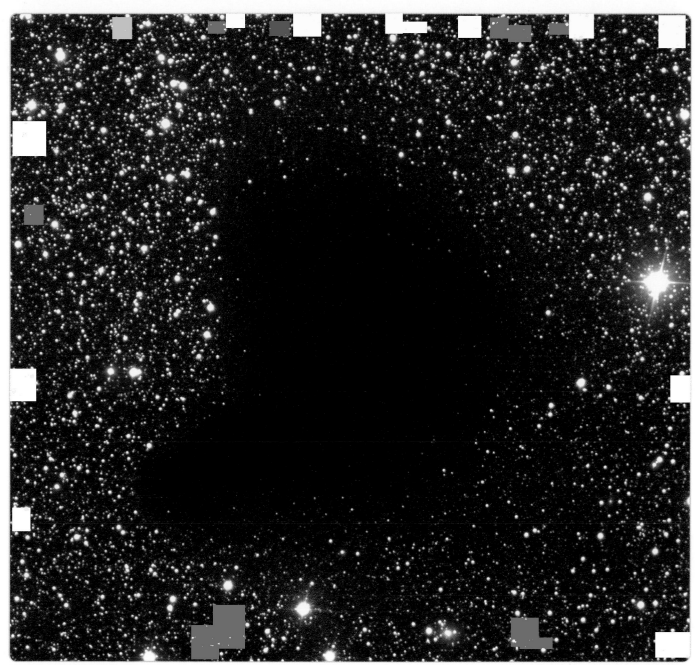

VLT/European Southern Observatory

Infrared View of Saturn

I f the mass of the neutrino were not precisely tuned, there would be no Earth-like planets and hence no life as we know it. We are indeed the children of stardust, stardust powered on its journey through the cosmos on the wind of neutrinos.

SHARON BEGLEY
The Hand of God

NGC 7635, The Bubble Nebula—*The "bubble" on the right is actually the smallest of three bubbles surrounding massive star BD+602522, and part of gigantic bubble network S162. As fast-moving gas expands off BD+602522, it pushes surrounding gas into a shell. The energetic starlight then ionizes the shell, causing it to glow. The Bubble Nebula is located in Cassiopeia.*

AURA/NOAO/NSF

Hubble Space Telescope/NASA/ESA

I don't think you can be up here and look out the window as
I did the first day and see the Earth from this vantage point,
to look out at this kind of creation and not believe in God.
To me, it's impossible—it just strengthens my faith.
I wish there were words to describe what it's like.
. . . truly awesome.

JOHN GLENN
Broadcast from the Discovery
Space Shuttle on November 1, 1998

SN1987A in the Large Magellanic Cloud—*Supernova remnant surrounded by inner and outer rings of material is set in a mass of ethereal diffuse clouds of gas from the destruction of a massive star. Astronomers in the southern hemisphere witnessed the brilliant explosion of this star on February 23, 1987. The many bright stars nearby are about 12 million years old, about the same age as the star that went supernova. The region appears to still be a fertile breeding ground for new stars.*

The human mind is not capable of grasping the Universe.
We are like a little child entering a huge library.
The walls are covered to the ceilings with books
in many different tongues. The child knows that
someone must have written these books.
It does not know who or how.
It does not understand the languages in which
they are written. But the child notes a definite plan
in the arrangement of the books
. . . a mysterious order which it does not comprehend,
but only dimly suspects.

⊹   ALBERT EINSTEIN   ⊹

Cygnus in the Milky Way—*The bright star Deneb (upper left of center) reveals the stars, nebulae, and dark clouds along the plane of our galaxy near the Northern Cross. Deneb is the brightest star in the constellation Cygnus, located in the tail of the Swan, and marks one side of the "Great Rift" in the Milky Way, a series of dark obscuring dust clouds.*

John P. Gleason

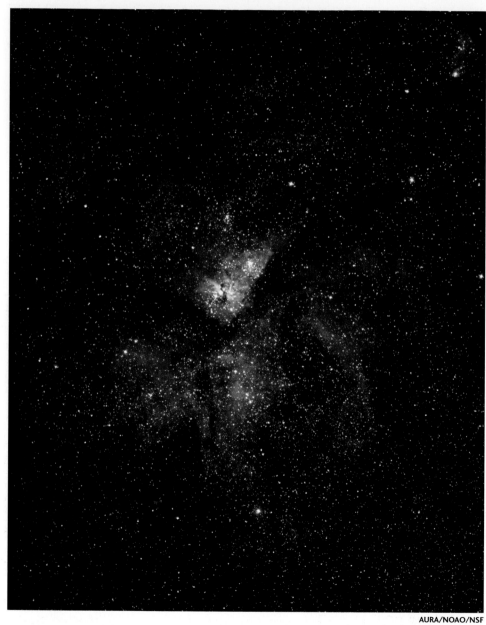

AURA/NOAO/NSF

The trend is to look for God in dramatic discontinuities in physics or biology, and if none are found, to declare religion vanquished. But God may act in subtle ways that are hidden from physical science.

JOHN POLKINGHORNE
President of Queens College at
Cambridge University,
a physicist for 25 years
before becoming an
Anglican priest.

Eta Carinae Nebula NGC 3372—*This gaseous bright nebula surrounds the variable star Eta Carinae, which attracted attention as early as 1840 due to one of the spectacular explosions that has characterized its final centuries. The Eta Carinae Nebula is about 9,000 light years away from Earth and can be seen with a small telescope in the southern skies in the constellation Carina.*

That which is, is
far off, and deep, very
deep; who can find it out?

ECCLESIASTES 7.24

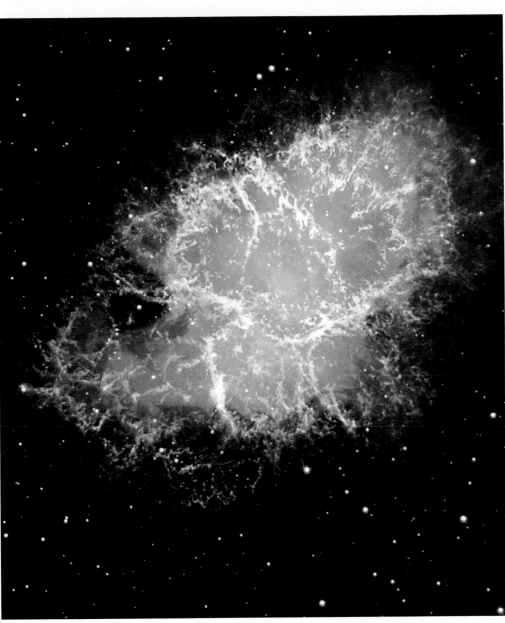

The Crab Nebula—*This spectacular super-nova explosion was recorded by Chinese astronomers in 1054 AD. The mysterious fil-aments appear to have less mass than expelled in the original supernova and higher speed than expected from a free explosion. It con-tains a neutron star at the center that spins 30 times per second around its axis. The Crab Nebula is about 6,000 light years from Earth.*

VLT/European Southern Observatory

127

I find it as difficult to understand a scientist who does not acknowledge the presence of a superior rationality behind the existence of the universe as it is to comprehend a theologian who would deny the advances of science. And there is certainly no scientific reason why God cannot retain the same relevance in our modern world that He held before we began probing His creation with telescope, cyclotron, and space vehicles.

WERNHER VON BRAUN
Creation: Nature's Designs and Designer

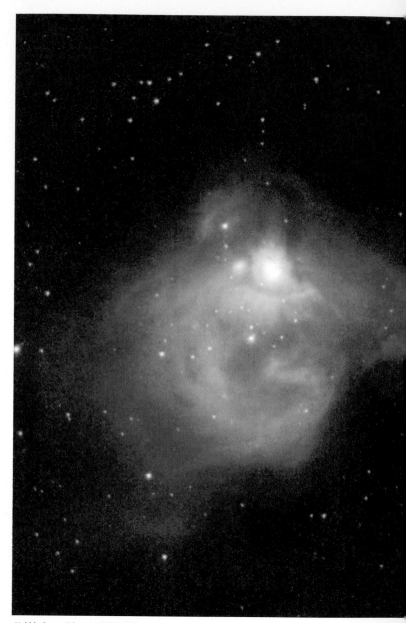

Massive Infant Stars—*The Hubble Telescope captured this rare image of young, massive stars as they are born and emerge from their pre-natal molecular cloud. Young stars evolve rapidly and are hard to find at this critical stage. They are usually shrouded from view by large quanities of dust, and can only be viewed when they emerge from their "cocoon."*

Hubble Space Telescope/NASA/ESA

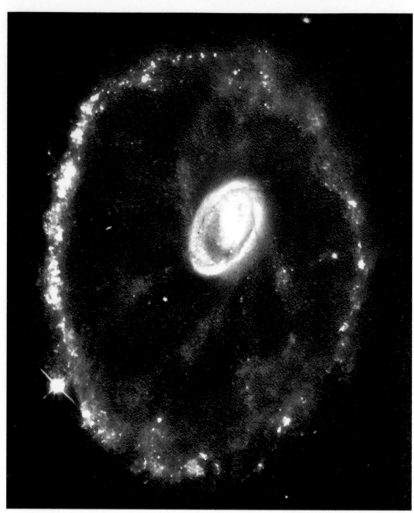

Cartwheel Galaxy—*Though originally a normal spiral galaxy much like ours, the striking ring-like feature of the Cartwheel Galaxy is the result of a smaller galaxy that careened through its core approximately 200 million years ago. The collision created a firestorm of new star creation, shown in the bright blue knots (gigantic clusters of newborn stars) and immense loops and bubbles blown into space by exploding supernovae. The Cartwheel Galaxy's ring is 150,000 light years across, large enough for our entire galaxy to fit inside, and is located 500 million light years away in the constellation Sculptor.*

Deep sky is, of all visual impressions, the nearest akin to a feeling.

SAMUEL TAYLOR COLERIDGE
Notebooks

In the dark time, the eye begins to see.

THEODORE ROETHKE

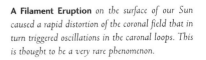 W hy, if we evolved on this earth alone and have known no other, do we sense a kinship between the mountains of Earth and the mountains of Mars, and find beauty in the stars?

TIMOTHY FERRIS
SpaceShots

A Filament Eruption *on the surface of our Sun caused a rapid distortion of the coronal field that in turn triggered oscillations in the caronal loops. This is thought to be a very rare phenomenon.*

TRACE/NASA

Oh! in his rapture he was weeping even over those stars, which were shining to him from the abyss of space, and he was not ashamed of that ecstasy. There seemed to be threads from all those innumerable worlds of God, linking his soul to them, and it was trembling all over in contact with other worlds . . .

FEODOR DOSTOEVSKI
The Brothers Karamazov

Watching satellites and staring at the stars, I seemed to lose contact with my earth and body and to spread out through the cosmos by means of an awareness that permeates both space and life—as though I were expanding from a condensation of awareness previously selected and restricted to the biological matter that was myself.

CHARLES LINDBERGH
Autobiography of Value

The Black Hole Powered Core *of glowing vapors is shown in this image of a unique and powerful active Galaxy. This nearby (13 million light years) galaxy known as Circinus, belongs to a class of mostly spiral galaxies called Seyferts, which have compact centers, and are believed to contain massive black holes. Circinus is also thought to have an Active Galactic Nuclei (AGN). AGN have the ability to remove gas from their centers by blowing it out into space at phenomenal speeds.*

Hubble Space Telescope/NASA/ESA

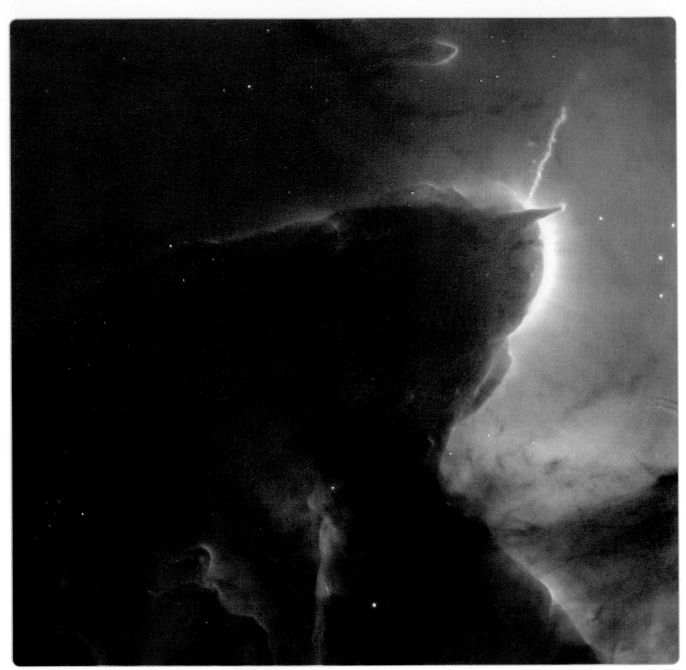

Hubble Space Telescope/NASA/ESA

E veryone takes the limits of his own vision for the limits of the world.

✛ ARTHUR SCHOPENHAUER ✛

Trifid Pillars and Jets—*A huge, dense gas and dust pillar in the Trifid Nebula is punctuated by a smaller, fingerlike pillar pointing to the right and an unusual jet shooting up. The pink dots are newly formed low-mass stars. A star near the small pillar's end is slowly being stripped of its accreting gas by radiation from a tremendously brighter star situated off to the upper left. The source of illumination for the jet on top which extends nearly a light-year is hidden. As gas and dust evaporate from the pillar, however, the hidden stellar source of this jet will likely be uncovered, possibly over the next 20,000 years. The Trifid Nebula is about 5,200 light years away, in the constellation Sagittarius.*

P Challis/CfA/Whipple Observatory

Remember that we can always look backward in time by looking out farther into space with our telescopes. The farther into space we look, the closer to the beginning we come.

STEPHEN HAWKING
Stephen Hawking's Universe

Hubble Space Telescope/NASA/ESA

Most Distant Galaxy in the Universe—*Appearing as a faint red crescent to the lower right of center, the galaxy in this image is the farthest known. The "gravitational lens" (the effect of a galaxy cluster so massive it warps space in its vicinity, allowing the light of a more distant object to curve around and be seen) is what brightens, magnifies and smears the more remote galaxy into a visible arc shape. The lensed galaxy's light reaches us from a time when the universe was only 7% of its current age of approximately 14 billion years, which places it 13 billion light years away from us.*
Globular Cluster M3 *(left)—This huge ball of stars predates our sun. Of the 250 or so globular clusters that survive in the Milky Way, M3 is the largest and brightest, easily visible in the northern hemisphere with binoculars. It contains about half a million stars, most of which are old and red.*

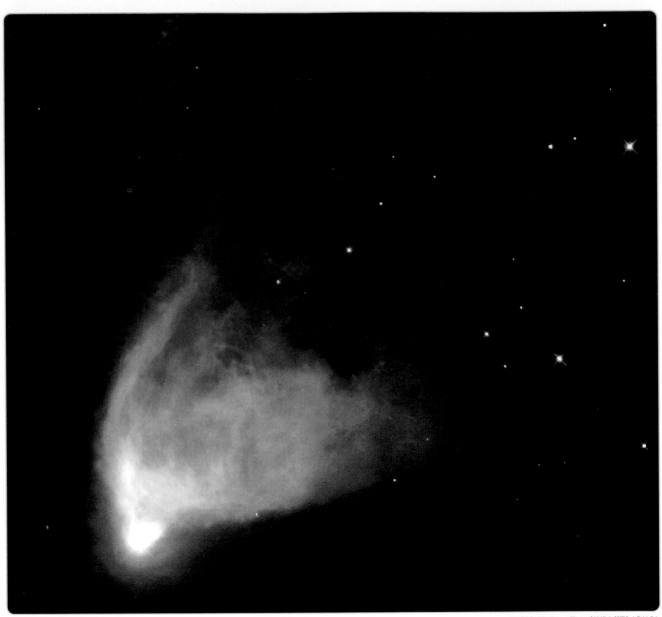

Instead of picturing God as a medieval monarch on a marble throne,
imagine God as the living awareness in the space between the atoms,
"empty" space that makes up about 99.99 percent of the universe.
Thinking of God that way gets us past some of the great
theological divides of the past. Is God immanent or transcendent,
internal or external, composed or compassionate?
Like the question of whether the atom is wave or particle,
the answer is: yes.

TOM MAHON
"The Spirit in Technology"

Hubble's Variable Nebula (NGC 2261) *was named after the American astronomer, Edwin P. Hubble, (like the space telescope) who carried out some of the first studies of this object. It is a fan-shaped cloud of gas and dust, illuminated by R Monocerotis, the bright star at the bottom end of the nebula. The star is about 2,500 light years from Earth, and has a mass about 10 times that of our Sun.*

The Universe begins to look more like a great thought, than a great machine.

✛ SIR JAMES JEANS

Stretched Spiral NGC 6872 *(left)—Measuring over 700,000 light years across from top to bottom, this is one of the largest barred spiral galaxies known. Its elongated shape may be related to its ongoing collision with a smaller galaxy, IC 4970, visible just above center. The spiral arm at the upper left exhibits an unusually high amount of blue star-forming regions. NGC 6872 is located in the constellation Pavo, 300 million light years away.*

Elliptical Galaxy NGC 1316 *(right)—The delicate, eerie dark dust lanes silhouetted against the glowing nucleus of NGC 1316 may represent the aftermath of a 100 million-year-old cosmic collision between it and a smaller, spiral galaxy. An enormous elliptical galaxy, it contains unusually small globular star clusters (visible as faint dots scattered across the image) that are too old to have been created by the recent collision and not bright enough to be typical of an elliptical galaxy. One hypothesis is that these globulars survive from an even earlier galaxy that was cannibalized by NGC 1316. The galaxy is 53 million light years away in the constellation Fornax.*

Hubble Space Telescope/NASA/ESA

W ho spread its canopy?
Or curtains spun?
Who in this bowling alley,
bowled the sun?

EDWARD TAYLOR
*God's Determinations
Touching His Elect*

Keyhole Nebula NGC 3324—*Created by the dying star Eta Carina, the dark and dusty Keyhole Nebula is a smaller region superimposed on its larger parent, the result of a violent outburst typical of Eta Carina's final centuries. An emission nebula containing much dust, the Keyhole Nebula is approximately 9,000 light years away, and was recently discovered to contain highly structured clouds of molecular gas.*

Knowing the plumbing of the universe,
intricate and awe-inspiring though that plumbing might be,
is a far cry from discovering its purpose.

GERALD L. SCHROEDER
The Science Of God

Penetrating so many secrets, we cease to believe in the unknowable. But there it sits, nevertheless, calmly licking its chops.

H. L. MENCKEN

Gas Emission *(left)—A filament of gas in the process of lifting off the surface of the Sun. The dark matter around it is about 20,000 degrees, while the hot kernels and threads around it are a millon degrees or more.* **30 Doradus** *(right) also known as the Tarantula Nebula (NGC 2070) is located in the Large Magellanic Cloud, about 170,000 light years away. It is one of the largest star forming regions in the Local Group of Galaxies.*

VLT/European Southern Observatory

There are many windows through which we can look out into the world, searching for meaning . . . Most of us, when we ponder on the meaning of our existence, peer through but one of these windows onto the world. And even that one is often misted over by the breath of our finite humanity. We clear a tiny peephole and stare through. No wonder we are confused by the tiny fraction of a whole that we see. It is, after all, like trying to comprehend the panorama of the desert or the sea through a rolled-up newspaper.

JANE GOODALL
Through a Window

Omega Nebula—NCG 6618, *also known as the Swan Nebula, the Horseshoe Nebula, and the Lobster Nebula, this bright star-forming region is crisscrossed by clouds and lanes of opaque molecular dust and gas. Only the surface of a "blister" shines in visible light, where it is ionized by the ultraviolet light of massive, young stars, and where the light is not blocked by the surrounding dust. Omega is estimated to contain over 800 times as much material as the Sun and is located in the constellation Sagittarius. It is 17 light years in diameter, and between 5,000 and 6,000 light years away from Earth, inhabiting the same spiral arm of the Milky Way galaxy as its near neighbor, the Eagle Nebula.*

AURA/NOAO/NSF

Why should we demand that the universe make itself clear to us? Why should we care? . . . It is something about understanding the totality of existence, the essential defining reality of things, the entire universe and man's place in it. It is a groping among stars for final answers, a wandering the infinitesimal for the infinitely general, a deeper and deeper pilgrimage into the unknown.

JULIAN JAYNES
*The Origin of Consciousness
in the Breakdown of the Bicameral Mind*

NGC 2207 & IC 2163 *are a near-collision of two spiral galaxies as they pass each other. The larger galaxy NGC 2207 (on the left) is exerting strong tidal forces on the smaller (IC 2163) that is distorting its shape, flinging out stars and gas into long streamers stretching out a hundred thousand light years, towards the right side of the image. Eventually billions of years from now, they will merge into a single massive galaxy.*

Hubble Heritage Team/AURA/STScI/NASA

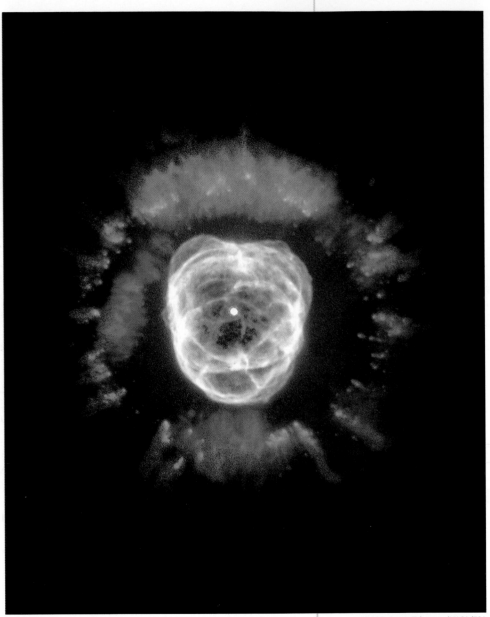

Hubble Space Telescope/NASA/ESA

. . . Every branch of human knowledge if traced up to its source and final principles vanishes into mystery.

ARTHUR MACHEN
The Novel of the White Powder

Eskimo Nebula (NGC2932)—*This planetary nebula, the glowing remains of a dying, Sun-like star, was first seen by William Herschel in 1787. It is about 5,000 light years away from Earth in the constellation Gemini.*

Hubble Space Telescope/NASA/ESA

Starburst Galaxy NGC 1808—*A tidal interaction with another nearby galaxy may explain the origins of the exceptional burst of star formation seen in this closeup of the galaxy's core. The star clusters (blue) can be seen amid thick lanes of gas and dust, with the brightest knot being a giant cluster of stars about 100 light years in diameter at center. The entire starburst region shown here is about 3,000 light years across.*

Tis very puzzling on the brink!
Of what is called Eternity to stare
And know no more of what is here than there.

LORD BYRON
Don Juan

Two things continue to fill the mind with ever increasing awe and admiration: the starry heavens above and the moral law within.

IMMANUEL KANT
Critique of Pure Reason

Veil Nebula—*A supernova explosion resulted in the fast-moving blast waves seen here; at the front of the waves, ionized gas in the supernova remnant rushes out, sweeps up material, then breaks up many atoms into ions and electrons. In 1993, astronomers found that the blue shockwave was catapulted away from the stellar explosion after the red shockwave, and has yet to catch up to it in some regions. The Veil supernova remnant has a very large, angular size—six times the diameter of the full moon. Different parts of it are known as the "Cygnus Loop."*

Hubble Space Telescope/NASA/ESA

This universe would never have been suitably put together into one form from such various and opposite parts, unless there were some One who joined such different parts together; and when joined, the very variety of their natures, so discordant among themselves, would break their harmony and tear them asunder unless the One held together what it wove into one whole. Such a fixed order of nature could not continue its course, could not develop motions taking such various directions in place, time, operation, space, and attributes, unless there were One who, being immutable, had the disposal of these various changes. And this cause of their remaining fixed and their moving, I call God, according to the name familiar to all.

ANCIUS MANLIUS SEVERINUS BOETHIUS, 480–575 A.D.
The Consolation of Philosophy
(written while in prison for heresy)

Massive Star Birth—*A turbulent cauldron of starbirth called N 159 is taking place 170,000 light years away in the Large Magellanic Cloud (LMC). Torrential stellar winds from hot, newborn massive stars within the nebula sculpt ridges, arcs, and filaments in the vast cloud, which is over 150 light years across. A rare type of compact, ionized "blob" has been resolved for the first time by the Hubble Space Telescope to be a butterfly shaped or "Papillon" nebula (upper left) buried in the maelstrom of glowing gases and dark dust.*

Hubble Space Telescope/NASA/ESA

Our ancestry stretches back through the life-forms and into the stars, back to the beginnings of the primeval fireball. This universe is a single, multiform, energetic unfolding of matter, mind, intelligence and life. All of this is new. None of the great figures of human history were aware of this. Not Plato, not Aristotle, or the Hebrew prophets, or Confucius, or Leibniz, or Newton, or any other world-maker. We are the first generation to live with an empirical view of the origin of the universe. We are the first humans to look into the night sky and see the birth of stars, the birth of galaxies, the birth of the cosmos as a whole. Our future as a species will be forged within this new story of the world.

BRIAN SWIMME
The Universe Is a Green Dragon

RCW38 —*This infrared image is of a region in the Milky Way about 5,000 light years away, where stars that have recently formed in clouds of gas and dust are still heavily obscured and cannot be observed with the visible part of the light spectrum.*

VLT/European Southern Observatory

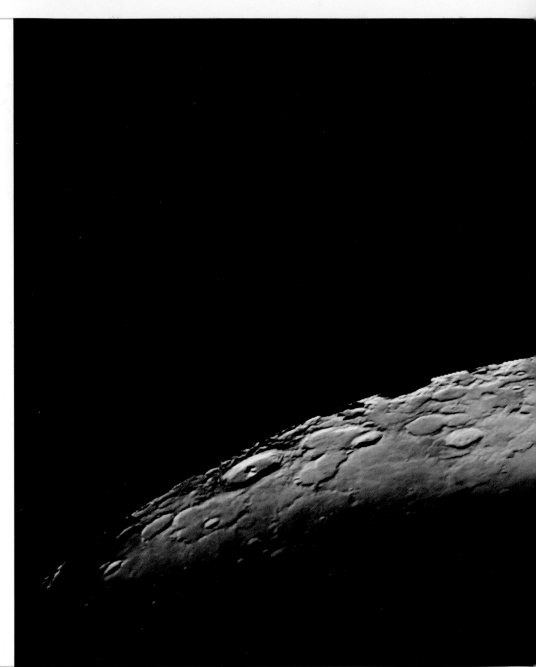

The Earth reminded us of a Christmas tree ornament hanging in the blackness of space. As we got farther and farther away it diminished in size. Finally it shrank to the size of a marble, the most beautiful marble you can imagine. That beautiful, warm, living object looked so fragile, so delicate, that if you touched it with a finger it would crumble and fall apart. Seeing this has to change a man, has to make a man appreciate the creation of God and the love of God.

 JAMES IRWIN
U.S. Astronaut

Earth & Moon—*This composite was made from a Galileo moon image and an image of Earth from Apollo 17.*

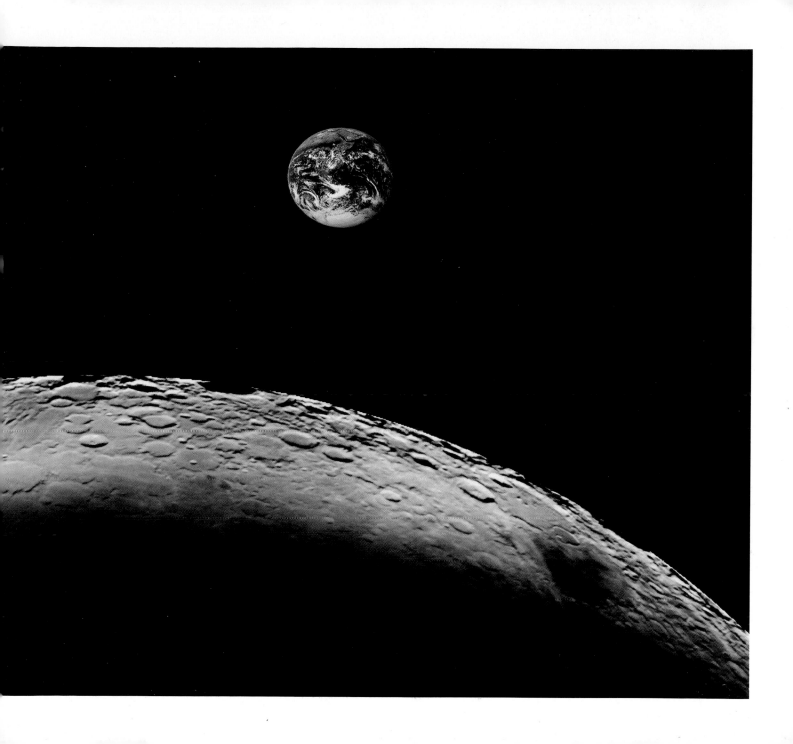

Jason Ware

To Alan Shepard
A genuine hero, who looked
back at Earth and wept.
You helped me understand.
We will miss you my friend.